NATURAL WONDERS
OF *Asia*

NATURAL WONDERS

OF *Asia*

THE FINEST NATIONAL PARKS OF
INDIA, THAILAND, THE PHILIPPINES & MALAYSIA

Biswajit Roy Chowdhury • Buroshiva Dasgupta • Indira Bhattacharya
Stephen Elliott • Nigel Hicks • WWF Malaysia

NEW HOLLAND

First published in 2004 by
New Holland Publishers Ltd • London • Cape Town • Sydney • Auckland

86-88 Edgware Road • London • W2 2EA • United Kingdom
www.newhollandpublishers.com

80 McKenzie Street • Cape Town • 8001 • South Africa

14 Aquatic Drive • Frenchs Forest • NSW 2086 • Australia

218 Lake Road • North Cote • Auckland • New Zealand

10 9 8 7 6 5 4 3 2 1

ISBN 1 84330 772 3

Commissioning Editor: Jo Hemmings
Editors: Deborah Taylor and Charlotte Judet
Designer: Gulen Shevki-Taylor
Cover Design: Gülen Shevki-Taylor
Cartography: William Smuts
Production: Joan Woodroffe
Reproduction by Pica Digital Pte Ltd, Singapore
Printed and bound in Singapore by Star Standard Industries Pte Ltd.

PUBLISHER'S NOTE
For ease of reference by the general reader, species are for the most part referred to by
their common names. In some instances, however, the scientific names have been used; and in a
number of others both the common and scientific names are given. The maps published in the
book are intended as 'locators' only; detailed, large-scale maps should be consulted when
planning a trip. Although the publishers made every effort to ensure that the information
contained in this book was correct at the time of going to press, they accept no responsibility for
any loss, injury or inconvenience sustained by any person using this book.

Front cover: Seen from the agricultural area of Kundasan, Gunung Kinabalu, Malaysia,
dominates the skyline.

Spine: A green peafowl photographed in Huay Kha Khaeng, Thailand.

Back cover top: The dense deciduous dipterocarp forests in Huay Kha Khaeng, Thailand

Back cover bottom left to right: Domestic buffallo bathing in a waterhole in Gir National Park,
India; Long-tailed Macaques, one of six primate species confirmed present in Ao Phangnga Marine
National Park, Thailand; The Asian Short-clawed Otter in Palawan, the Philippines; Bulbophyllum
lobbii, a small orchid species, photographed in Kinabalu Park, Malaysia.

Page 1: The view from the summit of Mount Apo in the Philippines, across forest, Lake Venado
and Mount Talomo.

Page 2: An elephant safari in Corbett National Park, India.

Right: Sambhar at Raj Bagh lake in Ranthambhore National Park, India, with an 18th-century
pavilion in the background.

Page 6 left: Asiatic Lion cubs (*Panthera leo parsica*) relieve their thirst in the cool of the day in
Gir National Park, India.

Page 6 right: The dominant geological feature of the Krabi–Phangnga coastline, Thailand,
is what geologists call drowned karstland; dramatic pinnacles of limestone plunging into an
azure sea.

Page 7 left: A *Fromia* starfish, common inhabitants of Balicasag's coral reefs in the Philippines.

Page 7 right: The narrow, white-sand shore of Pulau Sipadan, Malaysia, is shaded by elegant
windswept palms.

CONTENTS

INTRODUCTION

From the heights of the Himalayas to the depths of the Pacific rim coral reefs, and from arid deserts to humid rainforests and the rolling ocean, the diversity of wildlife, landforms and climate across Asia is truly staggering. Scattered across four countries of South and Southeast Asia, the protected areas described in this book encompass much of that diversity, from the desert of Gir National Park in western India to the tropical rainforest of Taman Negara in Malaysia, and the coral reefs of Balicasag Island in the Philippines.

It is no surprise that the animal wildlife is hugely diverse; the western regions contain species that reveal a link with Africa and many of those in the east are either unique to specific oceanic islands or linked to the ancient forms of Australasia. The result is a great range of types that include the lions and hyenas of the western deserts and the orang-utans and Philippine Eagles of the eastern islands. Then there is the wealth of species beneath the sea, particularly around the Malaysian and Philippine coasts, that includes hundreds of species of sponges and corals barely known to science, as well as the more familiar dugongs, dolphins, sharks and turtles.

Above: *Male fiddler crabs, with one big claw, have brilliant colours that differ from species to species.*

Yet, despite this huge diversity there is also some considerable unity across this vast region. The majority of the terrestrial protected areas, including those described in this book, consist principally of tropical forest with some grassland included. Climate and soil have greatly influenced the plant species prevalent in these forests, ranging from the deciduous forests of the drier areas, through teak and sal forests in the more moist regions of India, to the gigantic dipterocarp trees of the extremely humid lowland rainforests of Southeast Asia, to the gnarled and stunted forests of the high mountain areas. Despite this wide plant diversity, the resulting forest and grassland habitats are sufficiently similar, which allows a range of animal wildlife, at least birds and mammals, to spread far and wide. Asiatic elephants, several species of deer, antelope, wild cattle and hornbills, as well as leopard and several sub-species of tiger, to name just a few, can be found across almost the whole region.

Sadly, however, many of these protected areas are increasingly remote islands of wildlife and greenery in an expanding sea of agriculture and industry as human populations continue to expand. Under massive pressure, many of them may only survive – along with their precious wildlife – if they can be shown to have immediate economic uses. Careful and ecologically-sensitive tourism development may be one of the most important ways forward to finding that use, allowing trails and accommodation to be constructed in certain sections of a protected area, generating a business that enables and encourages people to explore these beautiful environments and hopefully see some spectacular wildlife in their natural habitats. Not only will such development allow protected areas to justify their existence in economic terms, but hopefully they will help to promote further the cause of protecting these areas simply for their own beauty and invaluable biodiversity.

Opposite top left: *A magnificent male Green Peafowl displays by fanning out its tail feathers to attract a female. Perhaps 300–400 individuals survive along the lowland rivers of Huay Kha Khaeng, Thailand.*

Opposite top right: *Endau Rompin, in Malaysia, is famous for its Sumatran Rhinoceros, a few of which are still left here..*

Opposite bottom: *A trio of Moorish Idols swim past clusters of coral in the Philippines.*

INDIA

India's northern boundary is formed by the Western and Northeastern Himalayan mountains. On the foothills of the **Western Himalayas**, the area known as Patlidun comprises tracts of terai (forest tree/shrub species typical of the lower foothills) and bhabar (forest species typical of the upper foothills). The Patlidun is inhabited by traditional species such as Indian Elephant and Sloth Bear.

The **Northeastern Himalayan** region is wet and humid with an early monsoon and the Brahmaputra River flows through the Assam valley creating extremely fertile soils and a dense forests.

The Western and Eastern Ghats and the Nilgiri hills form rough boundaries for **Central India**. Extreme climatic conditions mean that moist and dry Teak forests mix with deciduous forests of Sal.

The **semi-desert** region is entirely different from the rest of the country with high temperatures, low humidity and low precipitation. This zone is filled with thorny trees but is rich in fauna including Tiger, Leopard (Panther) and bear.

The **eastern coast** features the mangrove swamp forests of the Sunderbans, which includes Jackfruit and Coconut Palm and holds the largest number of Indian, or Bengal, Tiger in the country, and the Gir forest in Gujarat, which is the last stronghold of the Asiatic Lion.

Peninsular India, or Deccan, covers a vast region. Two monsoons nurture tall, leafy tree species including Teak and Mahogany. The area is unique for its endemic fauna such as primates, Nilgiri Tahr and the Malabar Giant Squirrel.

Above: In many cases female Indian Elephants (Elephas maximus) do not carry tusks, and if they do, they are small and known as tushes.

11

CORBETT NATIONAL PARK & TIGER RESERVE

Jewel of the Himalayas

The ink-blue Shivalik ranges of the Himalayan foothills rising in the distance are touched by the mist and the golden rays of the sun. The first shafts of sunlight descend obliquely to a shimmering copper rivulet below, where there is a constant hiss of frothing and gushing water within the silence of the wild. This is Corbett National Park, once a 'hunter's paradise' but today perhaps one of the most fascinating of India's wild heritage areas. The country's first national park to be established (1936), it was originally named the Hailey National Park. It featured unique, lush green tracts of terai (lower forest tract) and bhabar (upper forest tract) on the Himalayan foothills but in its earlier days, this tract was better known for its man-eating tigers. By 1958 a decision had been made to rename the park in honour of the one-time hunter turned conservationist, Jim Corbett who had been inspired by the area to write about his earlier hunting days. His immortal works include *Man-eaters of Kumaon* and *Jungle Lore*, which he wrote in his later, more conservation-minded years.

Tracts of Himalayan Jungle

Corbett was the first national park to be incorporated in the Project Tiger scheme, in 1973. Today Corbett National Park and Tiger Reserve sprawls over an area of 1318 square kilometres (510 square miles) of undulating Sal (*Shorea robusta*) forest between the districts of Nainital and Pauri Garhwal in Uttar Pradesh, in northern India. In October 1991, a buffer zone was added to the park's area, consisting of just over 300 square kilometres (117 square miles). The additional expanses of natural land used to form part of the Kalagarh Forest Division, the Sonanadi Wildlife Sanctuary (part of the Ramnagar Forest Division), and the Terai Forest Division. The newly created park with its adjoining verdant acres today make up the sole surviving jungles of the Garhwal Himalaya.

The Ramganga River gushes from the Upper Himalaya, flowing for about 40 kilometres (25 miles) through the northern part of the forest-covered hills, creating some of nature's most dramatic landscapes. Visitors can catch glimpses of fast-moving shoals of Indian Salmon and 'Freshwater Sharks' (the Mahseer) over the pebbled riverbed of the clear but turbulent waters of the Ramganga.

A dam has been constructed at Kalagarh, and the reserve encloses part of this reservoir. It attracts numerous water birds like pintails, Northern Shoveller, Garganey, the Cotton and Lesser Whistling Teal, Wigeon, and many others. The reservoir serves as a waterhole for fauna during the hot and sultry summer days, and on winter mornings, Common Indian Crocodile (*Crocodilus palustris*) – also known as Marsh Crocodile – and the thin-snouted Gharial (*Garialis gangeticus*) can be

Above right: A gentle-paced elephant safari in Corbett.

Opposite: The Ramganga River flowing through Corbett's northern reaches contributes to the park's scenic beauty.

Location: Situated at an altitude between 120 and 400m (400 and 1250ft). Nearest railhead is at Ramnagar, about 19km (12 miles) southeast of the park. Nearest airport is at Pantnagar 50km (30 miles) away.

Climate: Summer temperatures soar to 40°C (104°F), while on winter mornings the temperature dips to 10°C (50°F).

When to go: November–May; visibility of wildlife is better in the drier summer. Park closed in monsoon season July–October.

Access: The Delhi-Moradabad National Highway connects the Kashipur-Ramnagar- Dhikala network of towns. Project Tiger headquarters at Ramnagar, the park's mandatory entry point. Bus services operate regularly along the Nainital-Kathgodam-Ramnagar-Dhikala route.

Facilities: Basic facilities at Dhikala (forest rest houses and log huts), which has a canteen and shop. Forest rest houses: Gairal, Sarapduli, and Bijrani, in the park. Hotels in Ramnagar: Corbett Infinity Resort (Tiger Tops), Corbett Claridges Hideaway, Corbett River Side Resort.

Wildlife: Indian Elephant population significant. January is best for birdwatching.

Visitor Activities: Hightly trained elephants take visitors into the forest at dawn and dusk.

Map labels

= TIGER SANCTUARY

Kanda Rest House
1035m
Delhi
Mumbai
N
Dhikala Rest House
386m
Ramganga
Khinanauli Rest House
Ramganga Reservoir
Gairal Rest House
Sultan Rest House to Ranikhet
Main Gate
Sarapduli Rest House
S h i v a l i k
Paterpani Rest House
Dhangarhi
Gaujpani Rest House
R i d g e
Garjia
Corbett National Park & Tiger Reserve
Malani Rest House
Main Gate
Kalagarh Dam
Kalagarh
Dhara
Jhirna Rest House
Bijrani Rest House
Dhela Rest House
Amdanda Gate
Lal Dhang
Ramnagar
Kosi

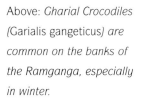

spotted on the banks of the Ramganga, basking in the gentler sun. They feed on fish in the dam, and are only dangerous to humans if approached closely.

Typical of terai-bhabar vegetation tracts, Sal is the dominant tree species. This thick Sal forest is interspersed with Shisam (*Dalbergia sissoo*), Jamun (Blackberry, or *Syzygium cuminii*), Khair (*Acacia catechu*), Ber (Indian Jujube), Mahua (Mowra Butter Tree), Rohini, and Haritaki. Further down the valley, clumps of spectacular rhododendron bloom in spring. The flowers of the Simal (Silk Cotton tree), Kachanar (*Bauhinia acuminata*), Palash (Flame of the Forest) and Amaltas (Indian Laburnum) bloom in abundance, creating a sylvan environment. Other floral species include the pink-flowered Foxtail Orchid, the Sariva orchid, Malajhan and ferns such as Hansaraj.

Above: Gharial Crocodiles (Garialis gangeticus) are common on the banks of the Ramganga, especially in winter.

Great Faunal Variety

The most distinct feature of this terai forest is the expanse of tall Elephant Grass which provides an ideal home for the larger carnivores. The park has *chauds* — vast, wild grasslands of the terai region that serve as grazing grounds for the herbivores, and are excellent places for viewing wildlife. The most prominent *chaud* is at Dhikala (the park's main base offering accommodation, but also acting as a good viewing site), which extends for an area of roughly 11 by 5 kilometres (7 by 3 miles). Other major *chauds* are Phulai, Khinanauli, Paterpani, Mohanpani, Bhadahi and Bijrani.

Below: In many cases, female Indian Elephants (Elephas maximus) do not carry tusks, and if they do, tusks are small – these are known as tushes.

The park has a great variety of wildlife. Cats include Tigers, Leopards (Panther), Jungle Cats and Leopard Cats. Corbett's population of 137 Tigers are notorious for avoiding human contact. Despite the fact that both Tigers and Leopards generally remain well-camouflaged within the dappled depths of India's forests, visitors with considerable patience do have the opportunity to see them. Visitors who spend at least three days in Corbett National Park are more likely to come across a Tiger.

An imposing denizen of the park is the Indian Elephant, large herds of which can be sighted at dawn and dusk during the summer season in the vast savannah of the Patlidun (valley), where the Ramganga valley has broadened out. A large population of Himalayan Black Bear and nearly 35 of the generally nocturnal

the Rhesus Macaque, which has a reddish face, can be spotted in the trees, while the Ratel (Honey Badger) and Indian Porcupine inhabit the dense undergrowth.

Reptile species such as the Barred Monitor Lizard, the deadly King Cobra – identifiable by the horizontal bands on its upper body – and the Indian Rock Python, a large, thick-bodied snake, inhabit the Corbett reserve. Otters delight in frolicking in the Ramganga River, which is also a breeding ground for fish such as the migratory Mahseer (a local freshwater shark) and Goonch (*Bagarius bagarius*). Nature lovers have petitioned the Uttaranchal government to declare the Ramganga belt a Mahseer sanctuary, in an effort to save the fish, which is presently endangered due to overfishing.

Sloth Bear also find sanctuary in the park.

Besides its reputation for its prolific wildlife, Corbett National Park is equally famous for sheltering Asia's largest deer numbers within its forests, and visitors are likely to come upon extensive herds of deer; a single herd can comprise hundreds of Chital (Spotted Deer). Other deer species to look out for are Sambhar, Barking Deer (Muntjac), and Hog Deer – a piglike deer of the grasslands and open forest. The coat of a Hog Deer is brown tinged with yellowish and reddish tints. At shoulder height, it stands 60 centimetres (24 inches) high, and has the habit of running with its head lowered, like its namesake the hog. These deer live on grass and leaves.

Of the smaller wildlife, the Common Langur, recognizable by its black face, silvery coat and long tail, and

A Magnet for Ornithologists

Corbett is popular among ornithologists and birdwatchers as 600 avian species have been recorded here. Some of the most notable birds include Kalij Pheasant, Peafowl (Peacock), Red Jungle Fowl, White-crested and Black Gorgetted Laughing Thrush, Mistle's Thrush, Indian Pitta, Paradise Flycatcher, and the White-capped and Plumbeous Redstart. Of special interest is the arrival of the Black-crested Cuckoo, which heralds the impending monsoon – the rains inevitably sweep through a week later after the cuckoo's arrival. Corbett counts an extensive number of raptors among its bird species, Blyth's Baza, Red-headed Merlin, ospreys, Crested Serpent Eagle, Scavenger Vulture, and the Hen and Marsh Harrier being only a handful. Wading birds include snipes, egrets and herons.

KAZIRANGA NATIONAL PARK

Conserving the Rare Rhino

Kaziranga's sprawling valley of 430 square kilometres (166 square miles) with its stretches of untamed landscape is situated in the state of Assam. An expanse of forest contiguous with the Mikir hills to the south and the turbulent Brahmaputra River to its north, it was accorded the status of a forest reserve as early as 1908. At this time, a law was imposed to restrict the ruthless shooting of rhinoceros, but by 1926 it was noted that the population had been further drastically reduced. Kaziranga was closed to visitors from 1930 to the end of 1937, and in 1940 it was upgraded to a wildlife sanctuary. Eventually, in 1974, Kaziranga was declared a national park.

Kaziranga's forests are known for their great biodiversity, comprising as they do mixed savannah grassland together with evergreen, moist deciduous and swamp forest.

Rhino – A Threatened Species

The park has recently become one of the last strongholds of the exotic Great Indian One-horned Rhinoceros, which during the mid-1950s was facing such an alarming decline of the species that numbers had dropped to about 12 animals. These vulnerable, short-sighted mammals are an easy target for poachers, who value their horns (which are, in fact, not of bone and keratin but rather composed of tightly compressed hairs) and which are used in powdered form for medicinal purposes in the Far East. In both India and Nepal, much of the rhino anatomy has some significance, whether aphrodisiac, medicinal or spiritual. Intense conservation efforts have increased the rhino population to approximately 1500 today. Rhinos are generally solitary animals, but can often be seen grazing on grass and leaves in the open grasslands. They enjoy muddy swamps, in which they submerge themselves. These animals have no predators, although Tigers and Leopards can be a threat to newborn calves.

Herds of Indian Elephant migrate between Kaziranga, the Darang district and the southern Mikir hills. Watching enormous families of elephants bathing in the rivers Diflu, Mora, Bhalukjhuri and Barjuri is an exhilarating experience for visitors. The total population is believed to be nearly 650.

It is unfortunate that due to the destruction of the corridors as a result of local tea cultivation, today the animals are being driven to seek out new habitats.

Above right: In the past, the Great Indian One-horned Rhinoceros (Rhinocerus unicornis) existed in many parts of India. As a result of extensive poaching, its occurrence today is limited to a handful of protected areas.

Opposite top: The vast swampy grasslands of Kaziranga are favoured by rhino, which wallow in the muddy waters.

Opposite bottom: Excursions into the park on elephant-back are leisurely and slow, but have their advantages: besides their elevated vantage point, visitors are also likely to get much closer to the wildlife.

Location: Golaghat district of Assam, the park lies along the main highway between Jorhat and Guwahati. Hamlet of Bokakhat lies to the east, 23km (14 miles) from Kaziranga. The park is flanked by the Bodo hills to the west.

Climate: Summer months are moderate (35°C/95°F) while winter nights are chilly (minimum of 7°C/45°F). Very heavy monsoon rainfall in summer (2300mm/90in).

When to go: November–March. Closed during monsoon season, mid-April to mid-October.

Access: Daily flights to Guwahati followed by drive to Kaziranga . Flights to Jorhat only twice a week. Bus services from Bokakhat to the park; car hire also available.

Permit: Apply to the Ministry of Home Affairs.

Facilities: Tourist information centre in Kaziranga. Jeeps are available within the park for drives at dusk. Accommodation in Kaziranga in forest rest houses and a tourist lodge owned by ITDC; canteen facilities. Comfortable accommodation at Wild Grass Resorts in Kohora.

Wildlife: Great Indian One-horned Rhinoceros, Asiatic Wild Buffalo, Mouse Deer and Barasingha.

Visitor Activities Early morning elephant rides can be booked in the park.

Seasonal Flooding of the Brahmaputra

Although the Brahmaputra River acts as a lifeline to civilization in the northeast Indian states, it causes great distress to Kaziranga's wild fauna when it floods its banks and submerges the forest floor. These annual floods inflict an enormous loss on deer, as well as smaller and and also larger mammals. Many of the park animals seek refuge in the Mikir hills of the Darang district, but unfortunately a large number are hit by heavy vehicles while attempting to cross the highways. After the flood waters subside, the soil is rich from the alluvial deposits and the forest floor is gradually transformed into an emerald-green expanse with the sprouting of new shoots which give rise to new plants, climbers and shrubs.

Above: *A watchtower near Kohra offers expansive views of the open grasslands.*

Above right: *The park guards make use of boats to patrol the park.*

Right: *The Indian Elephant (*Elephas maximus*) is smaller than its African counterpart, seldom exceeding a height of 3 metres (10 feet). What also sets it apart is its small ears, domed forehead and trunk ending in a single protrusion – in contrast to the African elephant's two protrusions.*

Prolific Birdlife

Kaziranga National Park protects as many as 325 avian species. Often the solitude of the forest is interrupted by the musical notes of the Hill Myna in the distant valleys and hills. Resident birds include Bengal Florican and the Adjutant Stork, while other prominent species are the Fishing and Crested Eagle, Sultan Tit, Collared Bush Chat, White-capped Redstart, Yellow and Pied Wagtail, Indian Lorikeet, Red-breasted Parakeet, Spotted Forktail and Blue Rock Thrush. Among the many waterbirds are large Cormorant, Lesser Whistling Teal, Bar-headed Goose, Merganser and Comb Duck.

Haven for Herbivores

Kaziranga is a vast wildlife refuge, and sustains large numbers of herbivores. One species is the Asiatic Wild Buffalo, or Water Buffalo (*Bubalus bubalis*), which breeds with domestic buffalo thus producing a hybrid race. The latter species is quite temperamental and often charges, unprovoked. The Manas National Park and Tiger Reserve is also home to this subspecies of buffalo. There are around 40 Indian Bison and many species of the deer family, including Hog Deer, Sambhar and Chital (Spotted Deer). The Softground Barasingha is one of Kaziranga's most highly endangered deer species (it is also present in Dudhwa National Park) and the park's monsoon-fed, water-logged terrain provides a very suitable habitat as its hooves are specially adapted to this environment. The elusive Mouse Deer is also a threatened species. The smallest of India's deer, standing 25 to 30 centimetres (10 to 13 inches) high, it is recognizable by the greyish horizontal stripes on its back. While cloven hooves are a characteristic of the deer family, the Indian Chevrotain has four well-developed toes on each foot instead, and the bones of the petty, or side, toes are completely formed. However, the male's antlers do not form.

Populations of Jungle, Leopard and Fishing Cat thrive, as do Wild Boar, Sloth Bear, Himalayan Civet, porcupines, pangolins, the Common Indian Hare, Common Indian Mongoose and Jackal. An animal that is striking in appearance is the Hoolock, or White-browed, Gibbon but these apes are not easily spotted in the hilly evergreen forests. They live as separate families of parents and young, forming groups of no more than six. Their diet is comprised of spiders, insects, fruits, and leaves from which they sip the dew.

Finally, nearly 50 Bengal Tigers and a reasonable population of Leopards (Panthers) survive in Kaziranga's jungles. Patient visitors will certainly have a chance of seeing Tigers in the forests.

Top right: *Located at different points in the forest, these guard posts help park officials keep a watch on poachers.*

Right: *Although the Sloth Bear (Melursus ursinus) is docile in appearance, it becomes an extremely ferocious animal if agitated, more so than the Tiger.*

Below: *The Mouse Deer, or Indian Chevrotain (Tragulus meminna), is the smallest member of India's deer family.*

KANHA NATIONAL PARK & TIGER RESERVE

Rudyard Kipling's Tiger Country

Famed as India's 'Kipling country' after the Indian-born English writer Rudyard Kipling who achieved renown with his *Jungle Book* stories only after his death, the Kanha National Park and Tiger Reserve is spread over the Maikal range of hills, part of the Satpura mountains in Central India whose daunting hills rise above 900 metres (3,000 feet).

The park comprises vast stretches of unbroken hilly forest on the Central Indian plateau in the state of Madhya Pradesh. It includes three forest ranges known as Kisli, Kanha and Mukki which are dominated by vast stands of tall Sal (*Shorea robusta*) and various *Terminalia* species; these are interspersed with well-watered valleys and flourishing grasslands.

Creating a sanctuary

A wildlife reserve was first established on the plateau in the Maikal hills in 1933, where the dry Teak zone of west Madhya Pradesh gives way to the evergreen moist Sal forests of the east. It also forms the catchment area of the Banjar River, which joins the Narmada at the town of Mandla to the north. The original park is bounded by a crescent-shaped hill range that rises to 900 metres (2,950 feet) for three-quarters of its extent and cradles open undulating meadows dotted with Sal and tracts of bamboo. Many of these meadows originated as clearings that were created by the Gond and Baiga aboriginal tribes of the area, through their practice of shifting cultivation. These meadowlands are locally known as *maidans*. Madhya Pradesh has undergone many physical

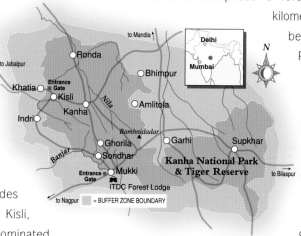

changes, the major contributing factor being the depletion of its mixed forests to the west and Sal forests to the east by felling for human settlement.

Kanha was declared a national park in 1955 at which time it comprised a forest tract of 250 square kilometres (95 square miles). It became a reserve under Project Tiger in 1973. Two more sanctuaries in the nearby Balaghat district, Maikal and Supkhar, were merged with Kanha in 1976. Today, the overall area is 1,945 square kilometres (745 square miles), of which 940 square kilometres (363 square miles) is the core zone.

From Barasingha to Tiger

The wildlife in Kanha is a good representation of the general diversity of India's fauna. Indian Bison, or Gaur, roam in large herds in the park. This is the most robust of India's bovine family, with some bulls standing 1.8 metres (6 feet) at the shoulder. Cows are slightly smaller. The colouring of the bull is jet-black with an ashy forehead and white stockinged feet, while females are brownish. They can occur at high altitudes of up to 1,830 metres (6,000 feet) where they exist on a herbivorous diet. The highest point in Kanha, known as

Above right: *The banks of Shrawan Tal are surrounded by Sal (*Shorea robusta*) forest.*

Opposite: Mahout-*led elephant rides take visitors to view Tigers once they have been located in the park.*

Location: The Mandla district of Madhya Pradesh State in Central India. The park is accessible from Jabalpur (170km/105 miles away) which also has the nearest airport and railhead. Nagpur is 270km (168 miles) from Kanha.

Climate: Summer temperatures are very high (maximum 43°C; 109°F) and winter is extremely cold (minimum 2°C; 36°F).

When to go: March–June. Park closed during monsoon from early July to late October. Closed midday to give respite to wildlife.

Access: Mandla is the district's main town (65km; 40 miles); buses between here and the park. The road from Nagpur to Kanha is bad; a car journey takes about five hours. Entrance gates at Kisli and Mukki, which have full canteen facilities. Food stores at Khatia, just beyond Kisli gate,.

Facilities: Forest Lodge managed by MPSTDC, forest rest houses, Baghira log huts of Madhya Pradesh (no self-catering required). Khatia has many private lodges, among them Kipling Camp, Krishna and Mowgli. Self-drive permissible with guide; jeep tours and elephant-back rides into Kanha. Khatia has an Interpretation Centre with displays and a sound and light show.

Wildlife: Tigers and Muntjacs often; Panthers rarely. Chausinghas and Nilgais, are also not often seen.

Visitor Activities: Walking the forested park and the rolling meadows. Watching the wildlife.

Right: *A male Soft-ground Barasingha (*Cervus duvauceli*) can be distinguished from the Hard-ground species by the outward and upward curve of its antlers.*

Below: *While hunting, Indian Wild Dogs, or Dhole (*Cuon alpinus*), generally move together in packs.*

Bamhnidadar ('dadar' translates as 'extensive plateau'), creates a suitable habitat for these Gaur. They have no predators, although their calves are sometimes attacked by Wild Dog, Leopard and Tiger.

Kanha is particularly well known for protecting a rare species of Barasingha, or Swamp Deer (*Cervus duvauceli branderi*), which has adapted to a hard-ground habitat in contrast to its marsh-living cousin (*Cervus duvauceli*). Variation exists in the antlers of the two species: on the hard-ground deer species, the main branch first curves backwards then forwards, bringing the points of the antlers parallel with the top of the head. On the soft-ground species, the main branch is set at right angles to the head, curving outwards and resulting in a wider spread of the horns. Hard-ground Barasingha inhabit the grassy plains, being less dependent on water, while their cousins are seldom out of water, thus preferring the marshlands. Breeding habits are similar between the two sub-species, and both generally feed till late in the morning and again in the cool evening.

The adapted deer sub-species exists only in Kanha National Park, while Soft-ground Barasingha occur in Uttar Pradesh and Kaziranga in Assam. The Barasingha population was at one point on the verge of extinction with a count of only 80 deer; conservation efforts adopted by the Forest Department in Kanha in recent years have led to its stabilization. Wild Boar and the Black-naped Hare also exist throughout the park.

Although famous for its Barasingha, Kanha is known better as Tiger country. The elegant beasts are spotted regularly here, even during the day. As in most tiger reserves, in the very early hours of morning the elephant riders, or *mahouts*, penetrate the interior of the forest in search of the elusive Tiger. When an animal is successfully tracked down, the *mahouts* escort visitors to it on elephant-back. Walking is not permitted in the park, and visitors are allowed in with their own vehicles only if accompanied by an authorized guide.

Other members of the cat family in the reserve are Panther (Leopard) and the smaller Jungle, Leopard Cat and Fishing Cat species. Another major predator is the Indian Wild Dog, or Dhole. These animals move in packs of between five and 25 and collectively hunt even the larger animals, such as Sambhar. The Dhole has the long, lanky body of a wolf, but its legs as well as its muzzle are shorter, and its ears rounded at the tips. It is glossy brown in colour, with a long bushy black tail.

Interestingly, Kanha's Jackal – which generally are

scavengers – are hunters. They move around in small families and kill Chital (Spotted Deer), small Sambhar and their fawns. Kanha's meadows are frequented by large deer populations where they graze in their hundreds. After the seasonal monsoon rains (July to October), the meadow grasses flourish, becoming tall and green and leading to poor visibility for animal viewing. During the dry season (March), the grasslands are often completely burnt as a result of forest fires, and the entire meadowland is thus cleared. Deer are then clearly visible, grazing at dawn and dusk.

Legend of the Lake

An historical legend surrounds a small lake in one of the reserve's meadows. Dating back to epic times, it recounts the story of a king named Dashratha, whose kingdom extended across the whole of the Indian sub-continent. He often hunted with bow and arrow, tracking his prey by listening intently for the sounds of animals. On day, while passing through a jungle, he heard what he thought was the sound of an animal drinking, so he shot at it. The next moment, he heard the sound of a man moaning in pain. He rushed to the spot to find a man named Shrawan; he had been hit by Dashratha's arrow and was dying. Shrawan had come to get drinking water for his blind parents, and the sound that King Dashratha had mistaken for an animal drinking was of a pitcher being filled with water. The king carried Shrawan's dead body to his parents and begged them for mercy, but they died on the spot after hearing of the demise of their only son. The legendary lake is today called Shrawan Tal ('tal' being the word for a reservoir).

Inset: *The Sand Boa (Eryse conicus) is a non-venomous snake; it is nonetheless deadly as its method of killing prey is by constriction.*

Below: *In the intense heat of summer, Tiger keep cool by immersing themselves in park waterholes and swamps.*

Avian Heaven

Kanha teems with avian life. Songbirds like the Racket-tailed Drongo and Magpie Robin enliven the forest with their sweet song, and before the monsoon arrives, Peacocks perform their spectacular displays throughout the forest. Two species of hornbill, the Common Grey and Malabar Pied, occur in large numbers. In winter, migrant birds such as Common Pochard, Lesser Whistling Teal and Black Stork congregate at the water-holes. Raptors spotted in the reserve are Shikra, Honey Buzzard, Sparrow Hawk, Lesser Kestrel, and the Crested Hawk and Crested Serpent Eagle, while several species of vulture, including the Long-billed and Scavenger Vultures, also make their home here.

Above: *The high surrounding plateau, part of the Maikal (hill) range, creates a watershed for the Banjar River flowing through the valleys below.*

Inset: *Of Kanha's eagle species, the Crested Serpent Eagle (Spilornis cheela) is the most frequently spotted.*

Clockwise from top left: *Species such as Common Pochard, Lesser Whistling Teal, Red-crested Pochard, Whistling Teal, and Black Stork are all migratory waterbirds that arrive in Kanha during the winter months to settle temporarily at the different wetlands.*

BANDHAVGARH NATIONAL PARK AND TIGER RESERVE

Ancient Stronghold of Many Kings

Bandhavgarh is the former land of valiant medieval kings – one-time bastion of the 12th-century Kalchuri dynasty – and is set in a vast expanse of verdant forest mantling the slopes around the ancient fortress, which used to belong to the maharajas of Rewa. The park is equidistant from the major towns of Madhya Pradesh State – Shahdol, Satna, Rewa and Katni – and rests in the cradle of the Vindhya hill range.

Declared a national park in 1968, with an area of 105 square kilometres (40 square miles), an additional 343 square kilometres (132 square miles) was added in 1982. It was brought under the protection of Project Tiger in 1994 when 245 square kilometres (94 square miles) of Panpatha Wildlife Sanctuary were merged with the existing national park.

The fort of Bandhavgarh dates back to Palaeolithic times (c. 4,000 years old) and features in the *Mahabharata* (an epic 3,000-year old Sanskrit poem), where it is referred to as Matsyadesh. During medieval times, the fort was ruled by various Buddhist and Hindu dynasties. Until the late 12th century, it was a stronghold of the Kalchuri and Baghel Hindu dynasties, but the Muslim rulers, the Lodhis, owned it temporarily. The fort's archaeological and mythological significance includes caves, rock paintings and carvings. There are also statues of the various incarnations of Vishnu, the Hindu god of stability. During the period when Bandhavgarh was under the domain of the maharaja of Rewa, the forests virtually became his personal game reserve.

Hills, Valleys, and Meadows

This country of 32 hillocks is crowned with flat plateaux and overhanging craggy cliffs. In turn, the hills are divided by green valleys and marshes, and the plains interspersed with meadows. The hills are composed mainly of permeable sandstones, allowing rainwater to percolate through. This has led to the formation of springs in the valleys and the marshes in the low-lying areas. Because of excessive water draining from the upper reaches of the park, some of the meadows have become marshland.

Perennial streams and rivulets such as Charanganga, Janad, Damnar, Umrar and Bhadar, with their crystal-clear waters, crisscross the region, promoting fertile green vegetation on the riverbanks. The area's combination of hills, rivers and valleys, meadows and marshes has created a unique biodiversity evident in the varied, luxuriant vegetation. Bandhavgarh's forests are mostly the moist deciduous type. The sheltered valleys are clothed with moist evergreen Sal forests, while drier slopes and plains are covered in mixed forest. Dense tracts of bamboo are scattered throughout the valleys.

The Chakradhara and Rajbahera meadows are major

Above right: Iridescent dragonfly Trithemis avrora.

Opposite: A female Chinkara (Gazella gazella) pauses beside the ancient ruins of Bandhavgarh fort; the population has unfortunately decreased considerably in these forests.

Location: Set amidst Vindhya ranges, altitude varies from 44–811m (144–2,660ft) above sea level.

Climate: Winter nights freezing (2°C/36°F), summer unpleasantly hot (maximum 42°C/108°F).

When to go: February–May; park closed July to end October.

Access: Khajuraho, 210km (130 miles) from park, is nearest airport; it is a five-hour drive from here to Tala (entry gate). Nearest railheads are Jabalpur (164km; 100 miles), Katni (102km; 63 miles) and Satna (112km; 70 miles) on the Central Railway and Umaria (32km; 20 miles) on the Southeastern Railway. Private bus and car hire available from Umaria (32km/20 miles), Amarpatan (80km/50 miles), Shahdol (97km/60 miles) and Rewa (105km/65 miles), as well as from Khajuraho and Satna.

Facilities: Accommodation provided by the MPSTDC (White Tiger Forest Lodge). Many private lodges at Tala (Bandhavgarh Jungle Camp – former Maharaja of Rewa's palace – and Tiger Trails). Visitors may enter park in own vehicles (petrol only, diesel is banned); or hire a taxi at Tala (park entry point). Park open from dawn to dusk. At entry gate, trained guides with interpretive skills can lead visitors through the park.

Wildlife: Tiger; Chital, Sambhar, Nilgai and Chinkara.

Visitor Activities: Elephant rides arranged by Forest Department.

Map labels: to Satna; Manpur; Dobka; Jungle Camp; Tala; Entrance Gate; Khilouli; Fort; Son; Dhamakhai; Delhi; to Umaria, Jabalpur & Katni; Mumbai; N; **Bandhavgarh National Park & Tiger Reserve**; Johilla; = SELECTED MOUNTAIN / HILL

Above: *Blue-tailed Bee-eaters are generally spotted in the park's tall-grassed meadows.*

Below: *Visitors pass through dense forests on their way to the Chakradhara meadow.*

features in the park, but uncontrolled grass growth at Chakradhara is threatening their survival. Valleys with deep, fertile soils thickly covered grasses are locally termed *vah*. Where these areas are marshy, they support tall grasses. An interesting species of the marshy meadows is the insectivorous plant *Drocera*. A small herb with a leafy stem of long, linear leaves, its fruit contains seeds that attract microscopic organisms. The park's grasslands mainly consist of the Saccharuphragmites, Themeda and Heteropogon species. The ground vegetation of the riverine areas is dominated by various species of bryophytes (characterized by moss and liverwort-type plants) and pteridophytes (characterized by ferns, horsetails and club mosses).

Sighting the Bengal Tiger

Bandhavgarh's rich floral diversity, constancy of food, water and shelter, and the strict monitoring and prevention of encroachment by humans from outside the park has promoted a wealth of animal life. As far back as medieval times, the area was believed to have supported a healthy population of Tiger – sometimes referred to in India as the Royal Bengal Tiger. The rare White Tiger used to occur here, but the last known one

Above: *A special quality of Bandhavgarh is that Tigers are often seen in broad daylight.*

Opposite: *Mahouts washing their domesticated elephants.*

was trapped in 1937 and there has been no report of a sighting since.

The chances of visitors spotting a Tiger in Bandhavgarh are greater than in any of India's other forests. In peak summer, these majestic striped beasts can often be seen at the waterholes of Chakradhara, Gopalpur, Barwanala, Jurmani and Jamunia. At dawn, trained elephants and their riders go into the forest to track the Tiger. Once discovered, visitors are led back to the sighting on elephant-back. Other important cats in Bandhavgarh are Panthers (Leopard), the Fishing Cat, Leopard Cat and Jungle Cat, and the rare Rusty-spotted Cat whose name accurately reflects its red-dappled coat.

As many as 34 mammal species have been listed for this national park and reserve. A huge population – more than 8,000 – of Chital (Spotted Deer) exists here, sharing the grasslands with Sambhar and (Muntjac) Barking Deer. Among the antelopes are Nilgai (Blue Bull) and Chinkara. Other major animals contributing to the wildlife diversity are Indian Wild Dog, Jackal, Wild Boar, Honey Badger, mongoose, porcupines and the Indian

Hare. Central India's most common monkeys, the Rhesus Macaque and Hanuman Monkey (or Common Langur), chatter and swing lithely in the treetops.

The park sustains over 70 species of butterfly with evocative names like Moon Moth, Common Rose and Blue Oakleaf. Shimmering dragonflies and damselflies are drawn to pools of limpid water.

The Bandhavgarh National Park has a longer 'season' than others because of a shorter monsoon. The diversity of its habitat is reflected by the wide range of birdlife: nearly 250 avian species have been reported. It provides a suitable habitat for different species of stork (White-necked and Lesser Adjutant) and hornbill (Malabar Pied and Common Grey), herons and cranes. It also provides a suitable habitat for tree-dwelling birds and birds of prey such as Crested Hawk, Crested Serpent Eagle, Honey Buzzard, Sikra, and Lesser Kestrel. In winter, the artificial waterholes of Bhadrashila, Gopalpur and Bathan attract migratory waterbirds like Nakta, Lesser Whistling Teal and Ruddy Shelduck. Smaller birds include Grey Tit, Baya Weaver Bird, Spotted Munia, the Green and Bearded Bee-eater and of the flycatchers, the Varditar, White-browed, Fantail and Paradise species, and Bandhavgarh's three species of parakeet: Alexandrine, Blossom-headed and Rosering. The Peafowl, with its spectacular tail-feather displays, adds its own blaze of colour to the jungle.

The Bandhavgarh National Park and Tiger Reserve is worth visiting for its breathtaking beauty alone. The three-day drive through the park takes in the Chakradhara meadow, the sprawling *vah* of Rajbahera, the tranquillity of Andheri Jhiriya, the forested hills of Badhaini, the wilderness of Ghoradaman, the spectacular view from the clifftops at Seshsaya and the coolness of the Jamunia stream.

Above: *From afar, the Black Ibis can clearly be identified by its scarlet crown.*

Inset: *Moon Moth.*

RANTHAMBHORE NATIONAL PARK & TIGER RESERVE

One-time Domain of the Maharajas

An awesome gift from Nature, the sprawling verdant forests of central India have, over the years, eventually been depleted and today, only a minuscule portion survives in the northwestern region. Before India gained Independence in 1950, the northwest was divided into several states that were under the domain of ruling Indian princes, or maharajas. They were merged into one state after Independence and came to be known as Rajasthan, the 'land of Rajputs'. The Rajputs, meaning 'sons of kings', were a military caste descended, according to legend, from the mythical warlike figure Kshatriya, and were renowned as great warriors from the seventh to the 12th centuries. They left behind them a rich legacy in terms of architecture and culture.

Princely states and dynasties

Ranthambhore National Park and Tiger Reserve lies in Rajasthan and memories of its regal past are evoked by the old turrets, mosques, wells, and other structures that are studded throughout the park. Overgrown with Peepal (*Ficus religiosa*) trees, they blend beautifully into their natural surroundings.

Originally a Hindu kingdom, with the fort established in 944AD, Ranthambhore came under Muslim rule intermittently over the next six centuries (increasing pressure from warring Arabs and Turks had eventually brought about Muslim power in much of northern India). The fort was taken over in 1301 by Ala-ud-din Khilji of the Bahmani dynasty, but the powerful Rajputs managed to regain control and Ranthambhore emerged as a powerful kingdom. During the 16th century, Muslim emperor Akbar was the most illustrious ruler of the Mughal dynasty which ruled India for more than 200 years. In 1569, in addition to Ranthambhore, Akbar took possession of the fort in Chittor, another princely state in Rajasthan, after 40 days of bloodshed between the Mughals and the Rajputs. The Mughals handed over the Ranthambhore fort to the Hindu rulers of the princely state of Jaipur, after which it remained with them until 1949, when Jaipur was merged with Rajasthan.

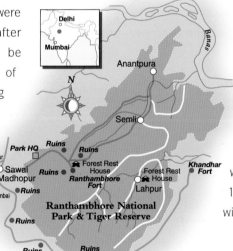

Above right: *A Tiger's angry snarl is sometimes difficult to distinguish from 'flehmen' behaviour, a wide-mouthed grimace that opens up an organ above the palate, which is covered with sensory cells, allowing Tigers to process scents.*

Opposite top: *Devotees come to pray for prosperity and everlasting union in marriage at the temple of Ganesh, situated on Raj Bagh lake.*

Opposite bottom: *Common Langur (Presbytis entellus).*

Opposite right: *This view of the Jogi Mahal, an old hunting lodge standing at the edge of Padam talao, can be seen from the ancient fort of Ranthambhore. It was built on the summit of a steep outcrop and offers sweeping vistas.*

Location: In the desert state of Rajasthan on the main Delhi-Mumbai railway line.

Climate: Summer (April–June) temperatures rise to 40°C (104°F). Winter nights are cold (8°C/46°F).

When to go: Winter (December–February) and March–April. Closed during the monsoon period; reopening on 1 October.

Access: Nearest town is Sawai Madhopur, which has a good bus service with many connections. Main Delhi-Mumbai railway line and is readily accessible from Jaipur (145km/90 miles). Sawai Madhopur, the nearest railhead and gateway to the park, is 11km (7 miles) away.

Facilities: Sawai Madhopur has excellent resorts and eco-lodges: Taj group-owned Sawai Madhopur Lodge (old hunting lodge of Maharaja of Jaipur); new Vanya-vilas, super luxury tented resort owned by Oberoi Hotels. Rajasthan Tourism Development Corporation (RTDC) manages more basic and functional Hotel Kamadhenu and Castle Jhoomar Baori Forest Lodge.

Wildlife: Tiger, Panther (Leopard), Hyena, deer, Sloth Bear, Wild Boar, and Jungle Cat. Prolific bird species.

Visitor Activities: Ranger-led safaris in open-sided jeeps and Canters (20-seater, open-roofed trucks); drives around picturesque reservoirs (good for photography).

Inset: *Mango fruits.*

While under the protection of the ruling maharajas of Jaipur, the forest and its animals were maintained as a private hunting preserve, where royal guests were entertained. It was to be an extremely positive move when, later, in 1972, the preserve was taken over by Project Tiger. The Ranthambhore National Park and Tiger Reserve extends across the Aravalli and Vindhya mountain ranges. The park was first established as a sanctuary in 1955, and became one of the first eight sanctuaries to fall under Project Tiger. In 1955 it was established that the forest covered an area of 410 square kilometres (158 square miles). In 1984, an additional 104 square kilometres (40 square miles) of adjoining forest were combined with the sanctuary, and named the Sawai Man Singh Sanctuary. It was at this time that it became a national park and tiger reserve.

The forests consist of deciduous trees, including the Dhak (Flame of the Forest), with occasional Renj, Ber (Indian Jujube), Sal, Mango groves, palms, and members of the fig family, the Banyan and Peepal. It is dominated by the massive battlements of Ranthambhore fort.

Ranthambhore has three artificial lakes (*talao*): Padam, Raj Bagh and Milak, all of which are essential because they supply water to the park's wildlife.

An estimated population of 38 Tigers prowl the Ranthambhore reserve. Over the last decades, as a result of the reserve's preservation policies, the Tigers have become more active during the day, and Ranthambhore is now well-known for frequent sightings of these cats in broad daylight. It is generally believed that Tigers are solitary, nocturnal creatures, but they appear to have undergone a change in this particular park and have become quite used to the sounds of human beings; they hunt during the day as well as at night. Common Peafowl, or Peacock, constitute a major prey species of this great cat. During the course of 1986, two tiger families were sighted and observed for a long time in jungle clearings, in daylight. One family with three cubs included a large male Tiger, which is very rare. Sighting one of these cats can never be an absolute certainty, but Ranthambhore has become a favourite haunt for wildlife photographers across the globe.

Right: *The aerial roots of* Ficus bengalensis

Left: *Ranthambhore fort rises above Padam talao; dating back to the 10th century, it belonged to Rajasthan's warrior people, the Rajputs.*

Inset: *The common Indian Monitor (*Varanus bengalensis*) is adept on both land and water.*

Below: *A common sight at the Padam and Raj Bagh talao are the egrets perched on the backs of Sambhars.*

Profuse Birdlife and Wildlife

The park supports a wonderful bird population. This includes Bonelli's and Crested Serpent Eagle, Great Indian Horned Owl, Tree-pie, Paradise Flycatcher, and Pheasant-tailed Jaçana, while in the lower-lying forest undergrowth are Grey and Painted Partridge, sandgrouse, quail, Red Spurfowl, and Common Peafowl. Waterbirds spotted in and around the lake are the Black, White-necked and Painted Storks, and spoonbills. A variety of ducks also migrate here from their Northern Hemisphere winter season.

Ranthambhore is also home to a large number of Leopard, which make up the second largest predator population in this forest. They are not as fearless as the Tiger, however, and sightings of them are infrequent. Other predators of Ranthambhore are the Striped Hyena, Jackal and Jungle Cat. Unfortunately Indian Wild Dogs were last sighted as far back as 1954.

Sloth Bears can be spotted in the Lakarda and Anantpura areas while driving through the park. In and around the lakes, Sambhar (India's largest deer species) are visible everywhere in large herds; Nilgai (Blue Bull) roam throughout the forests but their greatest concentrations are around the artificial lakes; and Chital, which graze on lush green vegetation, are drawn to the water in their hundreds during summer. Marsh Crocodiles, or Muggars, are often seen crossing from one lake to another. They prey on Sambhar, dragging the carcasses into the water even in daylight. Chinkara (Indian Gazelle), hares and mongoose can be spotted at the edge of the water, and Common Indian Monitors are frequently sighted.

A former hunting lodge, the Jogi Mahal, stands in a serenely beautiful setting overlooking the Padam reservoir, with the two other lakes, Raj Bagh and Milak, visible at the opposite end; the latter dry up in summer. These bodies of water attract a large number of Chital, Sambhar and Nilgai, which in turn attract Tiger. There are views of the park from Jogi Mahal, and a drive around the reservoirs is every photographer's dream.

SUNDERBANS NATIONAL PARK & TIGER RESERVE

Tigers in the Mangroves

The Sunderbans delta has been formed by the meeting of India's two great river systems, the Ganges and the Brahmaputra, which cross eastern West Bengal State and Bangladesh to drain into the Bay of Bengal. Created by sediments washed down from the Himalayas, it is the world's largest intertidal area – covering approximately 2,600 square kilometres (1,000 square miles) and is undoubtedly the most dynamic river basin that exists today. The Sunderbans is the largest prograding delta (constantly changing in a series of stages) in the world and holds the largest expanses of mangrove vegetation. In India, the Sunderbans covers an area of 4,264 square kilometres (1,660 square miles), defined by an imaginary demarcation line devised by (and named after) two surveyors, Dampier and Hodges, which extends in the north between the estuaries of the Hooghly River to the west and the Ichamati-Raimongol rivers to the east. The delta here is spread over two districts of 24 *parganas* to the north and 24 *parganas* to the south (a *pargana* is a subdivision of a district, generally containing many villages). The main trunks of both the Ganges and Brahmaputra cross Bangladesh to empty into the sea.

In 1973, the Sunderbans Tiger Reserve was established under the protection of Project Tiger with an overall area of 2,585 square kilometres (1,010 square miles) and a core zone of 1,330 square kilometres (520 square miles). In 1984, the area was proclaimed a national park and in 1985, the entire Sunderbans delta was designated a World Heritage Site. A buffer zone to the north of the park and tiger reserve contains a sanctuary of around 360 square kilometres (140 miles) called the Sajnekhali Wildlife Sanctuary.

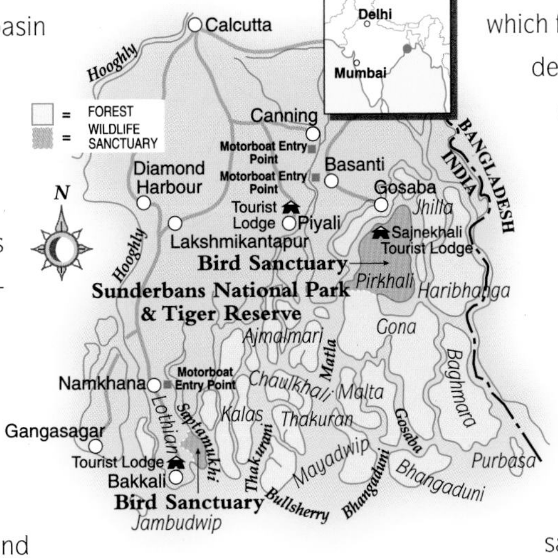

An Awe-inspiring Delta

The Hooghly River divides itself into innumerable streams to form narrow creeks which flow through the islands of this huge delta. Mudflats separate the creeks, some of which are very wide, while others are as narrow as canals.

There are 54 islands within the national park. Major branching streams traversing the Sunderbans have names like Matla, Bidyadhari, and Raimongal. This waterlogged habitat is regularly flooded and is characterized by its salinity and its intense humidity.

Above right: *Estuarine Crocodile (Crocodilus porosus), also known as Saltwater Crocodile.*

Opposite top: *Local fishermen paddle their sailing vessels, known in India as* dingi, *through the Sunderbans delta.*

Opposite bottom left: *Kankra (Bruguieria gymnorhiza), with its stilt-like roots, is a typical mangrove species.*

Opposite bottom centre: *A close-up view of the pneumatic root system of the region's mangroves.*

Opposite bottom right: *Muddy islands are covered with mangrove species, among them the Phoenix Palm.*

Location: In the Ganges deltaic region of eastern West Bengal. The nearest airport is in Calcutta, 112km (70 miles) from the Sunderbans. The nearest town is Gosaba, 50km (30 miles) away. There is a railhead at Canning.

Climate: Summer is very humid, (35°C/95°F) in December–February, while winter months are cool (15°C/59°F).

When to go: October to February is the best time to visit.

Access: There are several gateways to the Sunderbans: Canning is 48km (30 miles) from Calcutta and is well-connected by trains and buses; Basanti is 110km (68 miles) from Calcutta and is connected by buses. Boats to Sajnekhali from Canning or Sonakhali.

Facilities: Permission to enter the park by boat should be obtained from the Project Tiger office, Canning. Guides are provided at Sajnekhali Tourist Centre. Accommodation available in the tourist lodge (raised on concrete pillars) at Sajnekhali.

Wildlife: Different deer species, Estuarine (Saltwater) Crocodile and Gangetic Dolphin. Abundant sea- and waterbirds.

Precautions: The use of mosquito repellent creams and mosquito coils is advised.

Visitor Activities: Visitors can hire launches for guided tours and private excursions. Motorboats can be hired from different entry points to the park – Canning Basanti, Basirhat and Namkhana. Sajnekhali

Map labels: Calcutta, Hooghly, Delhi, Mumbai, FOREST, WILDLIFE SANCTUARY, Canning, Diamond Harbour, Motorboat Entry Point, Basanti, Gosaba, Jhilla, Tourist Lodge, Piyali, Sajnekhali Tourist Lodge, Lakshmikantapur, BANGLADESH, INDIA, Bird Sanctuary, Sunderbans National Park & Tiger Reserve, Pirkhali, Haribhanga, Ajmalmari, Gona, Namkhana, Motorboat Entry Point, Chaulkhali, Malta, Matla, Baghmara, Kalas, Thakuran, Lothian, Saptamukhi, Thakuran, Mayadwip, Gosaba, Purbasa, Bhangaduni, Gangasagar, Tourist Lodge, Bakkali, Bullsherry, Bhangaduni, Bird Sanctuary, Jambudwip

Heavy Southwest Monsoons

The region's main feature is a typical heavy monsoon season that experiences excessive humidity and lasts for almost half of the year. Summer in the Sunderbans stretches from mid-March to mid-June. The monsoon then arrives, brought by southwest winds, and lasts until September, though sometimes it extends to mid-October. The region gets intermittent rain all year round. Occasionally, cyclonic storms lash the delta during October and November, accompanied by high tides and waves that can cause great destruction.

December to February are the winter months, during which time the rivers become serene and quiet; it is perhaps the best period to navigate the delta's mangrove swamps. From April to May, violent thunderstorms known as 'Nor'westers' approach from the northwest. They are often accompanied by hailstorms.

Right: The Smooth-coated Otter (Lutra perspicillata) *frequents freshwater habitats – rivers, lakes and streams – where it feeds on fish.*

Below, from left to right: *The mangrove swamps provide a suitable habitat for the Mudskipper* (Periothalmus barbarus); *a Freshwater Turtle* (Pelochelys cantorii); *the female turtle will lay between 100 and 150 eggs in a protected hollow; at low tide, an army of crabs invades the exposed mudflats, among them the Fiddler Crab.*

Saltwater Mangrove Shores

Vegetation in the Sunderbans falls into the littoral forest type – mostly mangrove species growing in the shallow waters of the seashore. The lower tidal zones of the delta feature what are known as primary colonizers, the *Sonneratia* and *Avicennia* species, belonging to the saltwater mixed forest type and possessing submerged roots which bind the soil together; these roots tolerate high salinity. Above this tidal zone stretches an area characterized by the Rhizophora species, *Bruguieria* and *Excoecaria careops* forest, of which the Phoenix Palm is typical. The Rhizophora species, with their tangled aerial roots, are the most familiar of the mangrove trees. A mangrove of note is the Sundari from which the name Sunderbans is derived, in addition to the Hental, Baen, Goran, Golpata, and Passur species – in all, 64 species of mangroves occur in the delta.

Because the river system of this deltaic region is so interconnected with the Bay of Bengal's waters, high and low tide occur twice daily. During high tide, the entire mangrove forest – the highlands excluded – is submerged in water. When the tidal water recedes, it leaves soft alluvial soil behind.

Indian's Largest Tiger Population

The Sunderbans are famous for their Tiger numbers – the park boasts the highest population of this regal cat in India. Research shows that cubs are born after the rains, between February and May each year, and according to the last census, there are 273 Tiger in the park today. This predator has proved itself well able to adapt to any environment and the saline, waterlogged mangroves are no exception. Wild Boar and Chital form its staple diet but, unlike other parks of India, the Tigers also catch fish and crabs from the rivers in the delta to supplement their diet. The swampy environment indeed makes it difficult for Tiger to pursue their prey, and the proximity of human habitation to the animals' own habitat does cause conflict, so they do periodically become man-eaters.

Other wildlife species occurring here are the Rhesus

Macaque and the Fishing Cat. This stout, nocturnal cat is around 130 centimetres (4 feet, 3 inches) in length and has grey fur infused with brown. It lives near rivers, tidal creeks and reedbeds, preying on calves, fawns and – true to its name – sometimes fish.

Naturally, birdlife of the Sunderbans is characterized by water- and seabirds. Some of the more unusual species are Whimbrel, Goliath Heron, Large Egret (*Ardea alba*) and Median Egret (*Egretta intermedia*), Black-headed Gull, River and Whiskered Tern, Stone Curlew, Golden Pochard, and pintail ducks. The reserve has its share of raptors, among them White-bellied Fishing Eagle, Pallas's Fishing Eagle, and Brahminy Kite.

Turtles and Estuarine Crocodiles

The Sunderbans National Park harbours a few endangered reptiles, among them the Olive Ridley Turtle, which emerges from the Bay of Bengal to lay its eggs on shore. Another endangered reptile, the tortoise *Batagur baska*, is very rarely spotted.

In winter, huge Estuarine, or Saltwater, Crocodile (*Crocodilus porosus*) emerge from the cold waters to bask in the sun on the riverbanks. These carnivorous ocean-going reptiles, which grow to 6 metres (over 19 feet), swim as far as 64 kilometres (40 miles) out to sea. They lay between 25 and 90 eggs of which only 1 per cent survive. They have a life span of 25 to 50 years.

Aquatic mammals of the rivers and estuaries are the commonly occurring black, finless Little Indian Porpoise which has a rounded snout, as well as the Irrawaddy, Plumbeous and Gangetic Dolphin species. The latter is often sighted from boats in the upper streams, away from the estuary. A freshwater mammal, the Gangetic Dolphin is differentiated by its head which lengthens into an elongated beak. The young have pointed, conical teeth which become bony projections with age. They live in the rivers of the Ganges, Brahmaputra, Indus and larger tributaries, never entering the sea. The Common Otter is the sole aquatic carnivore of the delta.

Watchtowers are located within the tiger reserve, at Sajnekhali, Sudhanyakhali, Netidhopani, and Burirdabad. Visitors can hire launches, both for guided tours or private excursions, and motorboats from different entry points to the park – Canning, Basanti, Basirhat and Namkhana. West Bengal Tourism has established the Sajnekhali Tourist Lodge on Sajnekhali island, which also has a visitor centre with a nature interpretation facility.

GIR NATIONAL PARK

Last Stronghold of the Asiatic Lion

More than 2,000 years ago, the Indian (Asiatic) Lion played a role in Indian history even before the Tiger began to thrive on the subcontinent. The lion's vast habitat spread from southern Greece in the northwest to Palamau in the state of Bihar (now Jharkand) in eastern India.

Ashoka, one of the greatest of the Mauryan emperors, was in power from 272 to 232BC, and left a series of inscriptions with his edicts on pillars and rocks across India. Some of Ashoka's edicts describe the lion capital of Sarnath and these stand in north Bihar.

Ashoka became famous for his strongly expressed views on Buddhist pacifism, and his edicts encouraged his people to follow the code of dharma – that is, a moral, pious and virtuous life.

Before the focus on protection shifted to the Tiger, the Asiatic Lion was the national animal of India. Today it remains an emblem of the Republic of India.

Lion – A Threatened Species

The Asiatic Lion (also known as West Asian or Persian Lion, depending on its precise habitat), was fast disappearing from many areas of India at the beginning of the 20th century. The Gir forest in Saurashtra, in India's Gujarat State, formed part of the one-time princely state of Junagadh in India's pre-Partition days. The Lion of Gir were on the verge of extinction as a result of poaching and shooting; it was believed that not more than 20 Lion existed in Gir at the time. The rulers of Junagadh enforced a strict ban on the shooting of this cat and later, a limited quota of three animals per year was permitted to be shot at the discretion of the Nawab (Muslim prince) of Junagadh. These measures worked remarkably well and the Lion population subsequently increased. A census held in 1936 established a count of some 287 animals; a subsequent census indicates that the Gir forest holds a minimum of 175 but not more than 275 Asiatic Lion.

Today, Saurashtra's original Gir forest has shrunk from 3,070 square kilometres (1,195 square miles) to 1,150 square kilometres (444 square miles). In the mid-1900s, Gir was connected to the forest sectors of Girnar, Barda, Mitiyala, Alech hills, Dhank and Chorwad by corridors of forest, grassland and scattered hamlets. This enabled the Lion to roam freely throughout the region. It was during this period, in 1965, that Gir was registered a wildlife sanctuary, confining its existing cat population to the core sector of the forest. After acquiring this status, the subsequent implementation of the Gir Lion Sanctuary Project in 1972 aimed to protect the Asiatic Lion and its habitat as well as improve the living conditions of the Maldhari people. The sanctuary was upgraded to a national park in 1975.

Opposite: *Asiatic Lion cubs (Panthera leo parsica) relieve their thirst in the cool of the day.*

Above right: *Asiatic Lion* (Panthera leo parsica).

Map labels

to Junagadh
Dhari
N
to Keshod & Junagadh
Kamleshwar Dam
Kamleshwar
Sasan Gir
Kankai
Crocodile Breeding Farm
Entrance Gate
Gir National Park
Shirwan
Tulsishyam
Banej
to Una
to Veraval
Jamvala
= LION SANCTUARY BOUNDARY
Delhi
Mumbai

Sidebar

Location: In southwest region of the Saurashtra peninsula, Gujarat. Nearest airport is Keshod, 50km (30 miles) from the park. It is also accessible by rail from Sasan Gir (1km, or half a mile, from the park) on the Western Railway.

Climate: Summer temperatures are hot and humid (43°C/109°F); winter nights are freezing (4°C/39°F, at night; 24°C/75°F, during the day).

When to go: Closed from monsoon (June to September) till mid-October. A pleasant time to visit is December to May (although May is hot, wildlife viewing is good).

Access: Nearest town, Veraval, is 42km (26 miles) away. At a distance of 65km (40 miles), Junagadh is well-connected with Delhi and Bombay by train and bus. Buses and jeeps for hire at the Gujarat Tourism Office at Diwan Chowk in Junagadh.

Facilities: GSTDC-run Lion Safari Lodge at Sasan Gir village has canteen facilities and a dining hall. The deluxe Gir Lodge is very comfortable.

Wildlife: The only retreat in India of the Asiatic Lion. Also present, Panther, Striped Hyena, many deer species, Indian Wild Boar and Marsh Crocodile.

Visitor Activities: Guides are necessary in the park and can be hired at the entry gate. Visitors can take petrol vehicles (diesel not permitted) on prescribed routes only.

Asiatic Lion did also occasionally exist in the Girnar and Mitiyala forests and some coastal forest before the 1990 census. Here, too the situation has improved considerably, and prides of Lion are now permanently settled in these areas – at present, there are four independent Lion populations. In the past they were relocated to Gir but they repeatedly migrated back to the coastal forests in search of food and a permanent territory. They were finally settled here permanently after 1990.

Habitat of the Asiatic Lion

Page 38: *Asiatic Lion cubs (Panthera leo parsica) relieve their thirst in the cool of the day*

Above: *When it flies, the Indian Roller (Coracias bengalensis) reveals the dazzling blue on the underside of its wings.*

Below: *Domestic Buffalo grazing and bathing in the park's waterholes.*

Below right: *The Striped Hyena (Hyaena hyaena) generally prefers open country, where low hills and ravines offer shelter in protective hollows.*

The Asiatic Lion is no less majestic than its African counterpart, although there are some differences in appearance. The Indian species is much shaggier, its coat and the fringe of its belly are denser, and the hair of the elbow and tail tuft longer. The largest recorded Asiatic Lion measured about 2.9 metres (9 feet, 7 inches) in comparison with 3.2 metres (10 feet, 7 inches) for the African Lion. The Indian cat, however, inhabits only a tiny fraction of the vast territory that is covered by African Lion.

Unlike most wild cats, which are solitary animals, the Lion exists in groups, or prides. It spends up to nearly 20 hours sleeping during the day and may feed only once or twice in a week. In comparison with the Tiger, Lion were never present in as large numbers as the former cat, and were quick to fall prey to hunters. Disadvantages the Lion has versus Tiger are its need for open grassland habitat (Tiger are more adaptable and can also exist in dense forest and the shrubby semi-desert forests of the Aravalli hills) and it lacks the Tiger's crafty nature, essential for survival. The disappearance of open grassland and scrub forests, the rise in agriculture, improved firearms for hunters and encroaching human settlement throughout its territory are some of the factors which contributed to its extinction in other areas of India.

The Asiatic Lion can be observed at dawn and dusk. As these cats are not shy or fearful, visitors can watch them from their motor vehicles. But like all predators, sighting a Lion is not always guaranteed. There is a proposal by the Forest Department to set up a safari park in a fenced-off area of around 405 hectares (1,000 acres) to allow for easier observation.

Threat of human encroachment

One of the national park's major problems is its human population and their cattle herds. The herders of this

region, a tribe called the Maldhari, reside on the fringe of the sanctuary with the result that their domestic buffalo are prey to, and substantially reduced in number by, the park's Lion. The cattle population is estimated at 20,000; at the same time these domestic animals compete for food and territory with the wild ungulates. They have been known to spread disease among wild animals.

The Gujarat government has launched a scheme to try to relocate the Maldhari settlers, which involves building a wall around the sanctuary and providing them with new water sources outside the protected area.

Gir's other wildlife

Today, Gir's self-sustaining stable ecosystem nurtures over 450 plant species, 350 varieties of bird, 32 species of mammal, 24 kinds of reptile and more than 2,000 species of insect. Herbivores in the park – Chital, Chausingha (Four-horned Antelope), Nilgai (Blue Bull), Sambhar, Chinkara (Indian Gazelle) and Wild Boar – have risen in number from a total of 9,600 in 1974 to more than 38,200 in 1995. The smaller carnivores are Jungle Cat, Jackal, and Striped Hyena. Gir also shelters a large population of Panther (Leopard); they are seen here more than in any other national park. Their prey includes stray domestic dogs and the Maldhari's cattle.

The wildlife of the Gir forests is best viewed by touring in a jeep, as the roads are very rough for sedan vehicles. The best drives from Sasan, a park entry point, lead to sites named Baval Chowk and Kankai, Chodavdi, Tulsishyam and Kamleshwar dam.

A great number of Marsh (Muggar) Crocodiles bask in the rivers of Gir and particularly in the Kamleshwar dam. There is a crocodile breeding farm, popular with

visitors, at Sasan from where these reptiles are relocated to the lakes and rivers of Gujarat.

The park's vegetation consists of Dry Teak (*Tectona grandis*) and deciduous forest of Banyan, Jamun (Black-berry) and Flame of the Forest (also known as Palash or Dhak) as well as scrub of *Acacia* and *Euphorbia* species.

A variety of birdlife lives in the forests' tree canopies: Paradise Flycatcher, Black-headed Cuckoo, Grey Drongo, Pied Woodpecker, Coppersmith, Indian Roller, Crested Swift, Fish Owl, Black Vulture, Shaheen Falcon, and Bonelli's and Crested Serpent Eagle. On the forest floor are Painted Sandgrouse, Rock Bush Quail, Grey Partridge, and White-necked Stork.

The park has a sound infrastructure with good facili-ties. A forest bungalow and ITDC forest bungalow in the sanctuary require early prior reservation.

Above: *Domestic cattle in Gir's forest have become a serious problem, as they denude the grasses that act as grazing for the park's wild herbivores.*

Left: *The five-petalled flowers of Amaltas* (Cassia fistula).

NAGARHOLE NATIONAL PARK & WILDLIFE SANCTUARY

Tiger and Deer, Monkeys and Snakes

That the forests of south India are surviving today is quite unique – despite the fact that they occur parallel to the coast, they are flourishing along the high hills of the Western Ghats. The vast forests belonging to the Mysore plateau in the state of Karnataka stretch between the Western Ghats and the Nilgiri hills to the south. Karnataka's two national parks – Nagarhole (pronounced Nagara-holay) and Bandipur – are divided by the Kabini River, a tributary of the great Cauvery. Nagarhole is to the north of the river, while Bandipur lies to the south. The mountains mantled by their spectacular forests extend across into Mudumalai National Park in Tamil Nadu and down to Wynad Wildlife Sanctuary in Kerala State (Wynad actually extends along the western extent of all three parks, Nagarhole, Bandipur and Mudumalai).

About one-third of Nagarhole's area is designated as a Wilderness Zone, strictly prohibiting interference with the ecosystem in the form of forestry and tourism. The remaining portion of the forest has been developed into three Tourism Zones, with facilities for wildlife tourism; these are named Nagarhole, Karapura and the third, still in the planning stages, will be called Moorkal.

Due to their close proximity, Nagarhole and Bandipur have many similar features, but at the same time there are sharp contrasts in the weather, flora, mammals, reptiles, and birdlife. Nagarhole has an astonishing wealth of wildlife throughout its 640 square kilometres (250 square miles) of forest.

Tall-canopied Forests

Rainfall in Nagarhole is high, so its moist, deciduous forest is dense and abundant. The forest canopy is created by the tallest trees, which tower up to about 98 feet (30 metres). The upper-most canopy is dominated by the spectacular timber trees Mathi (*Terminalia tomentosa*), Nandi (*Lagerstroemia lanceolata*) and Tadasalu (*Grewia tilacfolia*). Two of the most expensive sources of timber are the dark Rosewood (*Dalbergia latifolia*) and Teak (*Tectona grandis*). The lower forest canopy is composed of fruit trees, which attract a great number of wild animals. Beneath this canopy, shrubs are dense and varied. Flowering shrubs like Lantana and Lupatorium grow profusely in the clearings created by logging.

Forest Fauna

Open grassy swamps in the forest, where the soil is perpetually moist, ensure that there are glades of succulent grass all year round. These attract ungulates such as Gaur (Indian Bison) – a common sight to visitors in the

Opposite: Indian Elephants in a mock fight at a waterhole; this is not aggressive behaviour, although it may appear so.

Above right: *The luxurious Kabini Tourist Lodge is perched on the bank of the picturesque river of the same name.*

Location: Mysore, at a distance of 90km (55 miles) away, is the entry point to the Nagarhole and Bandipur parks. The nearest airport is Bangalore (220km; 135 miles), while Mysore is the nearest railhead.

Climate: Nagarhole receives heavier rainfall than Bandipur (1600mm; 65in); there are two monsoons.

When to go: A favourable time to visit the park is between October and March (part-monsoon season, part-winter).

Access: The nearest towns are Kutta, 7km (4 miles) away, and Mysore. Buses run from both towns to the park. Car hire in Mysore and park itself.

Facilities: Book well in advance. Kabini Tourist Lodge offers accommodation in their lodge and in large tents with beds; located at the Karapura settlement (southern park entrance 5km/3 miles from here).

Wildlife: Indian Elephant, Tiger, Leopard (Panther), Sloth Bear, and four deer species. Excellent birdlife (250 species); viewing also by motorboat or coracles.

Visitor Activities: Guided jeep or van drives available at least twice a day. A park guard accompanies visitors and identifies wildlife for them. *Machaans* (watchtowers constructed from logs) near waterholes.

Map labels
to Hunsur
Mensur
Delhi
Mumbai
Sollepura
Murkal
Siddapura
to Mysore
Kalhala
Nagarhole National Park & Wildlife Sanctuary
Heggadadevan-Kote
Taraka Reservoir
Nagarhole
Nagarhole
to Kutta
Antarasanthe
Kabini Reservoir
to Gundlupet
to Ipatty
Kymara
Kabini Tourist Lodge
Karapura
Mastigudi
to Manatodi
Kabini

Above: *Nagarhole's grasslands are the favoured habitat of herds of Chital, or Spotted Deer (Axis axis).*

Nagarhole and Karapura tourist zones as they pass in their jeeps or vans.

Similarly with Bandipur, the forest is the ideal place to spot hundreds of Elephant, in both small and large herds, throughout the year. When summer (March to June) approaches, they range further in search of food and water. During this period, they can be best viewed on the banks of the Kabini River. Here, a large herd of these pachyderms, either crossing the river with their playful young or congregating at the riverbanks around sunset, is a familiar sight.

A Deer Haven

Four species of deer inhabit the park. Sambhar roam throughout the region in small groups, and are seen in such large numbers that one tends to take them for granted; the same goes for Chital, India's spotted deer. These beautiful animals gather in hundreds around the forest headquarters in the evening, and occur in clusters around the tourist rest houses, even in the late hours of morning. Muntjac (Barking Deer) can also be viewed from close quarters. This species has earned its name from its remarkably loud bark, not unlike that of a dog, which alerts others to any marauding predators. The Mouse Deer (Indian Chevrotain) is tiny and entirely nocturnal. As a result, these animals are rarely seen.

The Chausingha, or Four-horned Antelope, is the most remarkable ungulate of Nagarhole National Park. It is almost the size of a Muntjac but has longer legs. It is the only 'four-horned' antelope in the world – the male carries two regular horns, each of which has an extra projection extending slightly forward, creating the appearance of four horns. It is unfortunate that many of the park officials accompanying visitors on night drives fail to differentiate between this deer and the Muntjac.

Deer, Wild Dog and Tiger

Dhole (Indian Wild Dog) are prevalent in Nagarhole. Here, they prey on Sambhar and Chital. Smaller animal species are Wild Boar, Black-naped Hare (frequently sighted here), Giant and Flying Squirrel, and fruit bats. And if it's Sloth Bear visitors are after, these can be spotted in the Karapura Tourist Zone.

The treetops close to local settlements and tourist-designated zones (there is a greater abundance of fruits here) are the domain of the secretive and nocturnal Slender Loris, the Common Langur and Bonnet Macaque. The tiny Slender Loris (20 to 25 centimetres, or 8 to 10 inches, in height) sleeps in deep tree foliage during the day so is rarely seen by visitors. In appearance it has very large eyes ringed in black, proportionately large ears and a pointed snout; it has almost no tail. This primate is fond of Lantana berries, small birds, lizards, tree frogs, and small insects.

Although Bandipur Tiger Reserve counts as one of the original nine established under Project Tiger, it is in Nagarhole that one has the greater chance of coming across a Tiger, although the likelihood of sighting this cat in broad daylight is a lot less here than in some of the northern Indian parks. The latest census records around 50 Tigers. The elusive Leopard is also present, and in areas such as Karapura is sighted quite often. Among the smaller carnivores are Jackal, the Jungle, Leopard and Rusty Spotted Cat, Small Indian and Palm Civet, and mongoose. Sometimes, one will be lucky to encounter a group of Smooth Indian Otters (*Lutra perspicillata*) in the Kabini reservoir, which was created by damming the river in the 1970s; this reservoir separates Nagarhole and Bandipur. There are also Marsh Crocodile and Monitor Lizard here. Forest snake species include Rock Python, Krait, cobras, Rat Snake, Wolf Snake, and Russell's and Bamboo Pit Viper. Turtles and frogs are quite common.

The Nagarhole National Park, and particularly the Karapura Tourist Zone, is excellent for wildlife watching during the dry season of March to May. Guided tours in jeeps and open-sided trucks are popular. During the monsoon months of June to September and November to February, the forest is a rich, luxuriant green but the roads become slushy and muddy and sometimes visitors may be forced to remain in their rest houses.

Right: *Members of the Jenu Kuruba tribe; its people live in harmony with the surrounding forests of Nagarhole and have gained renown as honey-gatherers.*

Below: *A jeep travels along majestic bamboo-lined roads; open-sided jeeps afford visitors excellent wildlife viewing.*

PERIYAR NATIONAL PARK & TIGER RESERVE

A Sylvan Tract in the Western Ghats

In the quiet wilderness of the southernmost Western Ghats, in the state of Kerala, lies the sprawling Periyar National Park and Tiger Reserve. Historically, Periyar goes back a long way. In 1895, Periyar Lake had its beginnings under the guiding hand of the Maharaja of Travancore, who was an avid nature lover. The first game warden of the forests that currently make up Periyar was an S. C. H. Robertson, appointed by the maharaja himself. Delighted by the biodiversity of these forests, he developed the Nellikampathy Sanctuary, which in 1950 was eventually renamed the Periyar Tiger Sanctuary. It was later legislated to include a tiger reserve under the Project Tiger scheme in 1978, and today covers a vast expanse of 777 square kilometres (480 square miles). The Tiger habitat is concentrated in the core area of the national park (declared in 1982).

The last census confirms the population of these elegant cats at around 35 to 40, and visitors do spot them. Annually, 450,000 people visit the park.

The serene Periyar Lake stretches for 26 square kilometres (10 square miles) and is surrounded by waterways that have formed between the hills and islands. The dam constructed in 1895 was enlarged into a lake during British rule and provides a perennial source of water for the wildlife in the reserve. The national park is today surrounded by spice gardens and plantation estates. It has a recorded 1,936 floral species and possesses the only south Indian conifer, *Podocarpus*

wallichianus. In addition, 145 species of fragrant orchids bloom here.

From Lion-tailed Macaque to Flying Lizards

Periyar's sylvan environs offer a refuge to many mammals, reptiles and amphibians, and 316 avian species. The threatened Lion-tailed Macaque and Nilgiri Langur occur here, as does the Flying and Malabar Giant Squirrel. The elusive Nilgiri Tahr, which is present in the park, unfortunately is rarely spotted. Visitors can watch Indian Elephant swimming and submerging themselves in Periyar Lake. Large numbers – believed to be more than 1,000 – inhabit the forests. Periyar's herbivores – Gaur (Indian Bison), Sambhar, and Wild Boar – spend much of their time wandering along the lakeside, particularly during the dry seasons of March and April. They can be viewed from boat launches, which carry visitors on lake cruises. The lake carries a large population of turtles, among them the Travancore Tortoise and the Black Turtle. Leopard, Indian Wild Dog, Barking Deer and Mouse Deer

Above right: *The Flying Lizard* (Draco dussumeeri), *also known as Flying Dragon, lives in plantations of coconut and betel (a tropical flowering climbing plant).*

Opposite: Periyar Lake lies in the heart of the park.

Location: Set amid the high ranges of the Western Ghats in the state of Kerala. The nearest town is Kumily, 3km (2 miles) away.

Climate: Both summer (maximum 29°C/84°F) and winter (maximum 21°C/70°F) are moderate.

When to go: Between October and April.

Access: By road, head for Thekkady from Madurai (140km/87 miles) from the park, Tamil Nadu's temple town, then the district town of Theni. An hour's drive takes motorists to the Thekkady forest rest house in the hills. Beyond this is Periyar. Buses from Thekkady to the park; jeep hire available. By air from Cochin (200km; 125 miles). The nearest railhead is at Kottayam (114km; 70 miles).

Facilities: Accommodation in Thekkady forest house at the outer fringes of the sanctuary; Aranya Nivas Hotel in the park at the lake; Edapalayam Lake Palace and Periyar House, both near the lake. Lake Palace was once the summer residence of the Travancore royal clan. Resorts include The Spice Village and Taj Garden Retreat; Shalimar Spice Garden also worthwhile.

Wildlife: Great herds of Indian Elephant, Gaur, Wild Boar, Sambhar and other deer species. Also elusive Lion-tailed Macaque and Nilgiri Langur.

Visitor Activites: The Forest Department operates seven boats for cruising on Periyar Lake.

Map labels:

Aumill
to Madurai
Wildlife Preservation Office
Thekkady Park Headquarters
to Kottayam
Periyar House
Aranya Nivas Hotel
Edapalayam Lake Palace
Manakavala Rest House
Watchtower
1302m
Watchtower
Watchtower
Azhutha
1159m
Periyar Lake
Mullakady Rest House
1030m
Mullavar
Thanikudi Rest House
Watchtower
Periyar National Park & Tiger Reserve
to Moozhiyar
Delhi
Mumbai
Sabarimala Temple
Periyar
N

may also be spotted in Periyar. Visitors will see Common Indian Monitors sunning themselves on rocks, and should be watchful for Indian Rock Python and King Cobra which are prevalent here. Unusual species in Periyar are the Flying Snake and Flying Lizard which glide from the branches of trees. The former – slender and very fast but nonpoisonous – is 1 metre (3 feet) long with its black back beautifully marked by yellow or white cross-bands as well as speckles and red rosettes, while the latter is orange- or yellow-coloured.

The watchtowers are an excellent way to view the wildlife in the early mornings and twilight hours; these are situated at Edapalayam and Manakavala.

Kingdom fit for ornithologists

With its aquatic environment, protected nesting sites, and abundant fruits, berries, fish, and insects, Periyar provides the ideal conditions for breeding birds. This avian kingdom has attracted ornithologists from all corners of India and has been visited by legendary Indian ornithologist, Dr Salim Ali, to document its bird species. Darters, cormorants, ibises, and Grey Heron perch on dead branches projecting from the lake. In addition to these, kingfishers, the Racket-tailed Drongo, and the Great Malabar and Grey Hornbill frequent the waters.

Colourful butterflies and moths, carrying evocative names such as Common Crow, Indian Fritillary and Tamil Lacewing, hover over wildflowers such as the Lantana and Lupatorium species. Of these, the Atlas Moth (not endemic to India), is recorded in the *Guinness Book of Records* as the largest in the world; it can be spotted in the tiger reserve.

Rehabilitating Poachers

Of interest in the park is a recent eco-development project, the Thekkady Tiger Trail, undertaken jointly by the Forest Department and private sector. It offers visitors trekking with overnight camps led by armed forest guards, and poachers who have been reformed as naturalists and tour guides. Funds raised contribute to the livelihood of these former poachers.

Inset: *Atlas Moth*
(Attacus atlas).

Below and opposite:
Periyar lake was created by the damming of the forested valley, hence the dead tree stumps projecting from its waters. Tourist boats pass through spectacular forest tracts of the Western Ghats.

SOUTH CHINA SEA

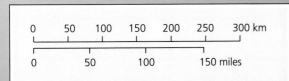

THAILAND

Central and Southeast Thailand are the country's most heavily developed regions. So it is perhaps surprising that Thailand's largest protected areas exist in the west of this region. The largest national park, Kaeng Krachan, is just three hours from Bangkok by car. Asian Elephants, and gibbons are the main attractions. Further north, the Western Forest Complex is Southeast Asia's largest forest with 14 contiguous protected areas. Huay Kha Khaeng and Thung Yai Naresuan Wildlife Sanctuaries, provide a last stronghold for Wild Water Buffalo and the fabulous Green Peafowl. In the Gulf of Thailand, Khao Sam Roi Yot has important coastal marshes and is a refuge for migrating shorebirds.

With mountain ranges, waterfalls and the highest regional forest cover, **Northern Thailand** is a rewarding destination for naturalists. Most of the northern parks are centred on individual mountains (doi) such as Doi Suthep-Pui, featuring hill walks and birdwatching. In the lower northern region, at Nam Nao and Thung Salaeng Luang, Asian Elephants, deer and wild cattle can be seen.

The Khorat Plateau, an undulating landscape, forms most of **Northeastern Thailand**. Khao Yai, at the western end of the Phanom Dongrak mountain range, is not only the nation's oldest park but also one of the most accessible, its abundant wildlife attracting huge numbers of visitors.

Dramatic coastal scenery, coral reefs and verdant forests draw millions of tourists to **Southern Thailand**. Limestone karst, pockmarked with gaping caves, is the dominant scenic feature and towers above both coastal and forest habitats. For rock climbers, Krabi makes a challenging destination.

Above: *The Dusky Langur is also called the Spectacled Langur due to the prominent white rings around its eyes.*

51

THUNG YAI NARESUAN– HUAY KHA KHAENG

Wildlife Sanctuaries and World Heritage Site

The combined wildlife sanctuaries of Thung Yai Naresuan and Huay Kha Khaeng comprise Thailand's most impressive conservation area and, indeed, the largest in mainland Southeast Asia. With a combined area of 6,427 square kilometres (2,481 square miles), these wildlife sanctuaries constitute the core of the Western Forest Complex, a vast collection of interconnected conservation sites that protect the best habitat for large herbivores, and their predators, and the most diverse range of birds, insects, reptiles and amphibians in the country.

Established between 1974 and 1991 and with an area of 3,647 square kilometres (1,408 square miles), Thung Yai Naresuan is the largest single

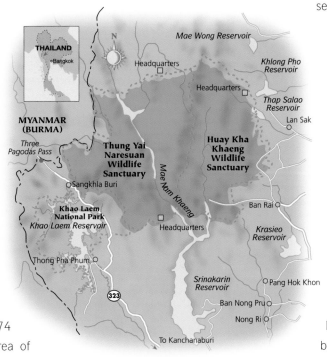

conservation site in Thailand. It is named after King Naresuan The Great who regained Siam's independence from Burma in the 16th century. Ranging in elevation from 100 to 1,811 metres above sea level (328 to 5,942 feet), it has recently been divided into two administrative units (an eastern one and a western one) for easier management. 'Thung Yai' means a large field, referring to vast open grasslands studded with cycads and trees on rolling hills at the centre of the wildlife sanctuary. These grasslands provide essential grazing for large ungulates and are maintained by frequent fires.

Huay Kha Khaeng is smaller at 2,780 square kilometres (1,073 square miles), and was established between 1972 and 1992. The sanctuary is hilly, ranging in elevation from 200 to 1,554 metres above sea level (656 to 5,068 feet) and, without the presence of villages within its boundaries, it is in a more pristine condition than Thung Yai.

A Diversity of Wildlife

Both sanctuaries contain a diverse range of forests, from deciduous dipterocarp forest in the lowlands to mixed deciduous forests at mid elevations and evergreen forests on the mountains and along the many streams and rivers that flow through the sanctuaries.

Opposite, above: *Dense deciduous dipterocarp forests make Huay Kha Khaeng one of the last strongholds for many of Thailand's largest mammals.*

Opposite, below left: *The elusive Clouded Leopard is one of seven cat species confirmed for Huay Kha Khaeng.*

Opposite, below right: *The main river through Huay Kha Khaeng is a vital habitat for the Wild Water Buffalo.*

Above, right: *The Grey Peacock-pheasant forages for fruits and insects on the ground in evergreen forest.*

Location: Northwest of Bangkok, in the provinces of Kanchanaburi, Uthai Thani and Tak. Extends west to Myanmar.

Climate: Monsoonal, mean annual rainfall 1,700 mm (67 in); rainy season May–October; cool season November–January (minimum 8°C/46°F); hot dry season February–April (maximum 37°C/99°F).

When to Go: Cool season for forest treks and birdwatching; early wet season for large herbivores.

Access: Access points to Huay Kha Khaeng reached travelling west from Uthai Thani and following Highway 3011 and turnoffs to Ban Rai and Ban Tai, or Highway 3282 to Lan Sak. Thung Yai via roads north from Kanchanburi–Sangkhla Buri Highway (323) near the Khao Laem Dam. Four-wheel-drive cars essential. No public transport.

Permits: Wildlife sanctuaries not open to the public, permits from Royal Forest Department in Bangkok or the Chiefs of the Wildlife Sanctuary Headquarters.

Equipment: Camping equipment, protection against mosquitoes and leeches, light clothes and strong shoes; warm clothing for the cool season.

Facilities: Tourist facilities not provided in wildlife sanctuaries.

Wildlife: Large herbivores, primates, large cats. Diversity of birds: Green Peafowl, Red-headed Vultures.

Visitor Activities: Forest walks, wildlife photography, birdwatching.

This wide range of habitats provides a refuge for Thailand's most diverse wildlife community. Although species lists for these sanctuaries are incomplete, Mahidol University's Conservation Data Centre lists 355 confirmed bird species, 85 mammals (including 14 bats), 45 reptiles and 23 frogs or toads for Huay Kha Khaeng. Confirmed species for Thung Yai Naresuan include 338 birds, 60 mammals (five bats), 27 reptiles and 13 frogs or toads.

Tigers and Other Predators

Thung Yai–Huay Kha Khaeng probably supports more Tigers than any other protected area in Thailand. Once widespread, Tigers have been reduced to probably no more than 250 individuals in tiny scattered populations. The Western Forest Complex is perhaps the last hope for survival of this species in Thailand, but even here, sightings are rare. These wildlife sanctuaries also provide a refuge to several other cats, including Fishing Cat, Leopard Cat, Jungle Cat, Clouded Leopard and Leopard, the Asian Wild Dog and the Asiatic Jackal.

Large Herbivores

Thung Yai–Huay Kha Khaeng abounds with the large herbivores required for the survival of the large cats. Three out of Thailand's four species of wild cattle live here. The

rarest of these is the Wild Water Buffalo and the 40–60 individuals that live along the rivers of the southern part of Huay Kha Khaeng may be Asia's last truly wild population of this species. Larger than the Domestic Water Buffalo, this group represents a genetic resource of incalculable value to agriculture in Asia, where buffaloes are the most important draft animals. Banteng, a close relative of domestic cows in Asia, and Gaur, a huge black forest ox, are the other wild cattle species in the wildlife sanctuaries. Thailand's fourth wild cattle species, the Kouprey, is now probably extirpated from the country.

Asian Elephants occur in small, scattered herds throughout the area and other endangered species of large herbivore, such as Malayan Tapir and Fea's Muntjak, can also be found there.

Birds

Thung Yai–Huay Kha Khaeng is a paradise for birdwatchers. These wildlife sanctuaries are the last strongholds of several rare bird species. Dependent upon riverine habitat are the highly endangered White-winged Duck and the magnificent Green Peafowl, the world's largest pheasant species. In the breeding season, male Green Peafowl attract females to open areas near streams with their trumpeting calls and fantastic displays of shimmering green tail feathers. The last resident pop-

Left: *Although it resembles the docile domestic buffalo, the Wild Water Buffalo is much larger, faster moving and more aggressive.*

Below: *A magnificent male Green Peafowl displays by fanning out its tail feathers to attract a female. Perhaps 300–400 individuals survive along the lowland rivers of Huay Kha Khaeng.*

ulation of perhaps a dozen Red-headed Vultures cling to existence in Thung Yai–Huay Kha Khaeng, the last remaining place in Thailand with enough carcasses of wild animals for them to feed on. Other notable rare birds include Kalij Pheasant, Grey Peacock Pheasant and Rufous-necked Hornbill.

The Rise of a Conservation Movement

In the 1980s, a famous environmental conflict in Thung Yai Naresuan triggered the growth of a powerful conservation movement in Thailand. The Electricity Generating Authority of Thailand proposed building the 187-metre (614-foot) high Nam Choan Hydroelectric Dam on a tributary of the Khwae Yai River. The reservoir formed would have divided the wildlife sanctuary into three separate fragments, destroying critical riverine habitats and disrupting migration routes. For the first time in Thailand's history, over 40 environmental groups united to oppose the dam. They were successful and paved the way for Thung Yai–Huay Kha Khaeng to be declared a UNESCO World Heritage Site.

However, this World Heritage Site is still under threat from many sources, including illegal trophy hunters and traders in wildlife products, forest fires, the presence of villages within the wildlife sanctuary and an expanding mining industry.

KAENG KRACHAN NATIONAL PARK

Thailand's Largest Park

Philip D. Round, one of Thailand's most eminent ornithologists, described Kaeng Krachan as 'the brightest jewel in the diadem of Thailand's National Parks'. He was not exaggerating. Not only does the park boast a bird fauna of at least 355 species, but it also retains thriving populations of large mammal species that have been severely reduced elsewhere. Among its 58 confirmed mammal species are Asian Elephant, Asiatic Black Bear, Malayan Sun Bear, Serow, Lesser Mouse Deer, Feae's Muntjak, Wild Dog, Asiatic Jackal, Malayan Tapir, Binturong, Malay Pangolin, Clouded Leopard and Tiger. The reason for the remarkably rich fauna of Kaeng Krachan is its vast

area of dense forest, including evergreen forest, mixed evergreen deciduous forest and deciduous dipterocarp forest, lying adjacent to a similarly large forested area in Myanmar. An extensive system of tracks and footpaths makes this park ideal for long-distance nature treks.

Established in 1981, Kaeng Krachan is Thailand's largest park, with an area of 2,915 square kilometres (1,125 square miles), of which an estimated 95 per cent is still forested. Situated just a three-hour drive southwest of Bangkok, it is also one of the most accessible places to see large mammals. The park is formed of rolling, forested hills, gradually rising westwards into mountains, reaching a maximum elevation of 1,207 metres (3,960 feet) at the summit of Khao Panoenthong. The western boundary of the park follows the international border with Myanmar.

Kaeng Krachan Reservoir

The park has been well protected because it is a vital water catchment area for the Kaeng Krachan Reservoir, created when Thailand's largest earth dam was constructed to provide electricity and irrigation water for agriculture. The area of the reservoir is 45.5 square kilometres (17½ square miles) and it includes up to 30 islands, depending on the water level. Many visitors

Opposite, top: The multi-layered forest canopy provides habitat for a wide range of primates and a host of birds.

Opposite, below left: The black fruits of the Pioneer treelet, Clerodendrum glandulosum, are edible by birds. They contain a powerful emetic used in traditional medicine.

Opposite, below right: The largest member of the civet family in Thailand, the Binturong is equipped with a long prehensile tail, which helps it balance in the tree tops.

Above, right: A juvenile Grey-headed Fish-eagle is one of many endangered bird species that can be seen.

Location: Phetchaburi and Prachuap Khiri Khan Provinces, southwest from Bangkok.

Climate: Annual rainfall 1,040 mm (41 in). Mostly June–November. Mean temperature 28°C (82°F). December–January (25°C/77°F), hotter March–July.

When to Go: November–February. Avoid public holidays.

Access: Four-wheel-drive vehicle essential; motorbikes and cycles not allowed. From Bangkok, follow Highway 4 to Phetchaburi, then to Thayang, turn right onto Highway 3187 and then 3499. Follow signs to Kaeng Krachan Dam. Park headquarters 4 kilometres (2 miles) beyond dam.

Permits: Bewildering system of permits. Purchase at park headquarters in office hours. Entry to the Panoenthong track is only allowed 5 am–10 am and 2.30 pm –3 pm and exits only during 12 noon–1 pm and 4.30 pm–6 pm. For information, call: 032-459-291.

Equipment: Light clothes and boots (warmer clothes if climbing Khao Panoenthong), insect repellent, full camping equipment and malaria/leech protection.

Facilities: Camping at Bankrang, Panoenthong, Tortip and park headquarters (and bungalows are for rent here); restaurant, visitor centre, information and guides for hire. Boats for charter.

Wildlife: Large ungulates, primates and large cats. Very diverse forest and water birds.

Visitor Activities: Treks, boat trips, caves and waterfalls.

Map labels: THAILAND, Bangkok, Kaeng Krachan National Park, Phetchaburi River, Kaeng Krachan Reservoir, To Tha Yang, Khao Panoenthong, 1207m (3960ft), Bankrang Camp, Hua Chang Cave, Park Headquarters, Sam Yoi, MYANMAR (BURMA), THAILAND, N

Above: *Kaeng Krachan is one of the few parks in Thailand large enough to sustain a small population of Tigers. These powerful predators favour dense forest, where they prey on mammals up to the size of Sambar and Banteng.*

Right: *Wild bees' nests can be found hanging from the branches of trees.*

come to Kaeng Krachan simply to relax on the shore of the reservoir, near the park headquarters, and enjoy camping, swimming and boat trips. Birds around the reservoir and its tributaries include Little Grebe, Chinese Pond Heron, Osprey, White-breasted Waterhen and up to ten different species of kingfisher. Along stream edges, Thailand's largest frog species, the Malayan Giant Frog, can be seen. However, the park's most impressive wildlife attractions lie 30 kilometres (18½ miles) west of the headquarters, where dense forest begins.

Exploring the Forest

A single-lane track to Panoenthong Camp, suitable for four-wheel-drive vehicles, a network of walking trails and several campsites enable visitors to penetrate deep into the forest, but tickets must be purchased at the park headquarters before beginning the journey.

Large evergreen trees dominate the forest canopy, including *Tetrameles nudiflora*, *Acrocarpus fraxinifolius*, *Elaeocarpus grandiflorus*, *Stereospermum fimbriatum*, *Barringtonia macrostachya* and *Crateva magna*.

Asian Elephants, Banteng and Leopards are often seen along the road at night. The Indochinese Leopards

of Kaeng Krachan have been studied by radio tracking. Lon Grassman, a researcher at Kasetsart University, showed that they range over 8.8-18.0 square kilometres (3 to 7 square miles) and eat mainly Hog Badger, Barking Deer and Common Wild Pig, all of which are abundant in the area and likely to be seen at night.

One of the easiest ways to view wildlife is to camp at Bankrang, 15 kilometres (24 miles) along the Panoenthong track from the entry checkpoint, and walk quietly along the main track and footpaths at dawn or

Above, left: *Sun Bears are equally at home on the ground or in trees, where they feed on bees' nests and fruit, and construct nests from small branches.*

Above, right: *Asian Elephants are sometimes seen at night along the road to Panoenthong Camp, but the visitor is more likely to come across tracks or droppings than the animal itself.*

Right: *A* Drynaria rigidula *fern grows on a large evergreen forest tree that dominates the forest canopy. This epiphytic plant grows on tree trunks and branches and absorbs nutrients from rainfall and detritus trapped by its fronds.*

Right: *The Blue-winged Pitta is a common breeding visitor at Kaeng Krachan during the rainy season.*

Far right: *This epiphytic orchid (Rhynchostylis coelestis) has found a precarious root-hold on the trunk of a tree. Such orchids do not penetrate their 'hosts', but use their support to gain a place in the sun.*

Below: *The Indochinese Leopards of Kaeng Krachan have been the subject of intensive scientific study that has provided detailed information on their behaviour and dietary habits.*

dusk. In the morning, White-handed Gibbons rouse campers with their penetrating songs, whilst crashes in the forest canopy betray the presence of Banded Leaf-monkey, Dusky Langur and macaques (Pig-tailed, Stump-tailed and Long-tailed). From Bankrang, forest rangers guide visitors to Hua Chang Cave, aptly named after one of its limestone formations, which strongly resembles the head of an elephant.

Parasitic Plants

Botanists will be interested in several rare parasitic plants that grow nearby, such as *Sapria himalayana*, in the same family as the world's largest flower, *Rafflesia*. Feeding on the roots of lianas, this curious plant develops buds the size of baseballs or cricket balls, which push through the leaf litter and open into bright red flowers shaped like 10-pointed stars, covered with white spots. The flowers smell like putrid meat to attract the carrion flies that pollinate them. Several *Balanophora* species, which parasitize tree roots and look more like fungi than flowering plants, are also common in the area.

Birdwatcher's Paradise

Birdwatchers may spot up to six species of hornbill, eight barbets, 15 woodpeckers, seven broadbills and five pittas.

Left: *The early morning songs of White-handed Gibbons are often heard around the campsites of Kaeng Krachan. They live in family groups and their songs warn off neighbouring families from invading their territory.*

Below: *The Woolly-necked Stork has been extirpated from most of Thailand, but a few individuals remain in Kaeng Krachan, preferring marshes and pools in more open areas of forest.*

Some of the rarer bird species include Grey-headed Fish-eagle, Blue-rumped Parrot, White-fronted Scops-owl, Barred Eagle-owl, Plain-pouched Hornbill, Olive-backed Woodpecker, Brown-chested Flycatcher and Ratchet-tailed Treepie. The latter is a recent new record for Thailand, previously known only from northern Vietnam, Laos and southern China. The park is also one of the last refuges for the endangered Woolly-necked Stork.

Long-distance Nature Adventures

For hardy adventurers an overnight trek to the highest point in the park (the summit of Khao Panoenthong) provides a good chance of sighting Asian Elephant, Gaur, Banteng and Sambar Deer. The ascent starts from the Panoenthong campsite at 'Km 30' on the main track. It takes at least six hours to complete the 10-kilometre (6-mile) climb. At the summit, campers rising early in the morning are rewarded with spectacular views of forested valleys blanketed in clouds, which slowly evaporate as the sun warms the atmosphere. From Khao Panoenthong summit treks of several days can be undertaken to Tortip Waterfall, a cataract with 18 steps, and along the Phetchaburi River, passing hot springs along the way. Guides from the park headquarters are essential for all these treks.

KHAO SAM ROI YOT MARINE NATIONAL PARK

Coastal Marshes and Limestone Pinnacles

A diversity of habitats, striking scenery and spectacular caves are the main attractions of Khao Sam Roi Yot, Thailand's first marine national park. Declared in 1966, the park consists of a long, narrow, isolated, jagged limestone mountain, rising from an alluvial plain to 605 metres (1,947 feet) above sea level, overlooking coastal marshes and beaches. The precipitous topography has protected both forests and remnant mammal populations. The park was enlarged in 1982 to include internationally important freshwater marshes, but it is still relatively small at only 98 square kilometres (38 square miles). A literal translation of the park's name is 'Mountain with 300 Peaks'. Visitors can enjoy a wide range of activities here, including spotting rare migrant birds, boating through mangrove forest, scrambling through awe-inspiring caves, or relaxing on a tropical beach.

Marshlands of International Importance

Khao Sam Roi Yot is of particular interest to ornithologists. At least 316 bird species have been recorded in the park, of which 150 are migrants. Near

Opposite: The coastal wetlands of Khao Sam Roi Yot are of international importance for bird conservation, but the park is also one of the most endangered in Thailand.

Above, right: The Purple Heron prefers to frequent the coastal wetlands of Khao Sam Roi Yot's for stalking fish.

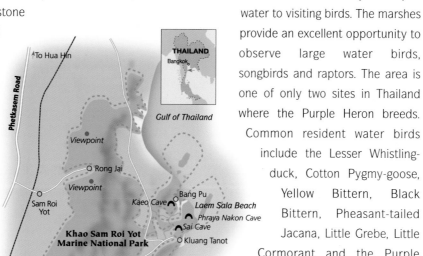

the village of Rong Jai, on the inland side of the mountain, are the best lowland coastal marshes in Thailand, consisting of reed beds, and a network of small pools and canals, which offer both security and open water to visiting birds. The marshes provide an excellent opportunity to observe large water birds, songbirds and raptors. The area is one of only two sites in Thailand where the Purple Heron breeds. Common resident water birds include the Lesser Whistling-duck, Cotton Pygmy-goose, Yellow Bittern, Black Bittern, Pheasant-tailed Jacana, Little Grebe, Little Cormorant and the Purple Swamphen.

The marshes provide a crucial refuge for winter migrants, flying south from China and Siberia to escape the cold, including several species of duck (of which Garganey is the most common), Grey Heron, Eurasian Marsh and Pied Harriers, Greater Spotted and Imperial Eagles, and passerines.

The IUCN *Directory of Asian Wetlands* ranks the site as globally important. Despite international recognition of the park's conservation value, however, it is one of the most threatened conservation areas in Thailand. Sadly, drainage and pollution have severely reduced the quantity and quality of water in the marshlands. Poaching of water birds, burning of reed beds, uncontrolled cattle grazing and the conversion of large areas into shrimp farms have severely damaged the area. It would be an international tragedy if this situation were allowed to continue.

Location: 63 km (39 miles) south of Hua Hin, in the province of Prachuab Khiri Khan.

Climate: One of the driest areas of Thailand. Mean annual rainfall only about 1,000 mm (39 in), mostly in the southwest monsoon in May–October, when high winds occur. Dry season December–March. Mean annual temperature 27°C (81°F).

When to Go: December to March best for winter bird migrants. The park becomes very crowded during public holidays.

Access: By car from Bangkok, follow Highway 4 to Pranburi. Turn left at Pranburi crossroads and follow signs 25 km (40 miles) to park entrance. Drive 14 km (22½ miles) to headquarters. Buses from Bangkok to Pranburi, where motorcycle taxis or buses can be hired.

Permits: Entrance fee charged.

Equipment: Protection against mosquitoes essential; torch for caves; swimwear for beaches.

Facilities: Bungalows and tents for rent at park headquarters, Laem Sala Beach and Sam Phraya Beach; restaurants at park headquarters and beaches. Accommodation available on private resorts near Bang Pu.

Wildlife: Serow, Dusky Langur, a wide range of water birds, limestone flora and mangrove forests.

Visitor Activities: Visitor centre and nature trails. Birdwatching, swimming and relaxing on beaches, exploring caves, boat trips through mangrove forest.

A Diversity of Shorebirds

Shorebirds are an added attraction for birdwatchers at Khao Sam Roi Yot. No other comparable coastal site supports more species within such a small area. On mudflats, common waders include Common Redshank, Common Greenshank, Marsh Sandpiper and Broad-billed Sandpiper. Spoon-billed Sandpipers and Little Stints can sometimes be observed among flocks of Rufous-necked Stints. Along sandy beaches, Greater Sand Plovers, Bar-tailed Godwits, Sanderlings and Terek Sandpipers are commonly seen. Little Terns and Malaysian Plovers nest on beaches above the high-tide mark, although disturbance by tourists, egg stealing and trampling by cattle undoubtedly destroy many nests.

Mammals on View

Tool-using monkeys provide an intriguing spectacle along the shoreline of Ko Khoram, one of several small islands within the national park. At low tide, Long-tailed Macaques scour the rocks for shellfish. The monkeys grasp small rocks, using them as hammers to crack open the shells and gain access to the nutritious meat inside. This unusual sight can be observed from boats hired from local fishermen. Visitors are not allowed to land on

the island or to feed the monkeys, to avoid disturbing this unique behaviour. Khao Sam Roi Yot is one of the best places to see another primate, the Dusky Langur. This delightful black-and-white monkey can easily be observed, moving through the mangrove trees around the park headquarters in the late afternoon.

The largest mammal surviving in the park is the Serow, a black goat-like animal that is superbly adapted to steep terrain. Serows can be seen with binoculars in late evening or early morning on the limestone crags. For a closer view, take the path from the park headquarters to the Khao Daeng viewpoint. Here, the Serow population appears to be fairly stable at around 50 individuals.

More elusive among the parks 14 confirmed mammal species are Common Barking Deer, Common Wild Pig, Banded Linsang, Fish-eating Cat, Malayan Pangolin, Malayan Porcupine, Leopard Cat, Slow Loris and possibly Leopard. Small-clawed Otters can sometimes be seen chasing fish in marshlands and mangroves.

Magnificent Caves

Undoubtedly the most impressive geological features of the park are its caves the most famous of which is Phraya Nakon Cave. This cave consists of two vast

caverns, open to the sky, with trees growing inside. Three of Thailand's kings have visited the cave and a royal pavilion, constructed for a visit by King Rama V in 1896, adds a majestic air to what is already an awesome natural feature. The pavilion is the symbol of Prachuab Khiri Khan. The cave is accessed from the small fishing village of Bang Pu. From there, a limestone promontory is traversed by a steep, but well-made, path leading down to Laem Sala Beach. Alternatively boats can be hired to ferry visitors around the promontory. From the beach, a further steep climb taking about half an hour leads to the cave's entrance.

Sai and Kaeo Caves are also worth a visit. Although smaller than Phraya Nakon, they are more highly decorated with stalactites, stalagmites and 'petrified waterfalls'. Guides with lanterns lead visitors to glittering calcite crystals.

Left: *The Dusky Langur is common in the mangrove forests around the park headquarters. This monkey is also called the Spectacled Langur due to the prominent white rings around its eyes.*

Above: *The Spot-billed Pelican is one of many endangered bird species that find refuge in the coastal marshes of Khao Sam Roi Yot.*

DOI SUTHEP-PUI NATIONAL PARK

Temples and Waterfalls

It is said that tourists cannot claim to have really visited Chiang Mai, Thailand's northern capital, unless they make the pilgrimage to the famous temple, Wat Pratat, at the heart of Doi Suthep-Pui National Park. Constructed in 1372 or 1373 AD, the temple's golden chedi, which houses a relic of the Lord Buddha, dominates the city, glinting in the sunlight on a sub-peak of the mountain, surrounded by forest. The mountain is named after the 7th-century sage Vasudeva (also called Rishi Warsuthep), a central figure in local mythology, who lived in a cave on the mountain.

Doi Suthep-Pui National Park was created in 1981 to protect not only the surroundings of the temple, but also the diverse forest ecosystems of the mountain, which provide a magnificent green backdrop to Chiang Mai city. The park consists of an isolated granite massif, with two main peaks. Doi Pui is the highest (1,685 metres, 5,528 feet), but the whole mountain is usually referred to as 'Doi Suthep', the secondary peak. Besides Wat Pratat, other cultural points of interest include the Hmong hill-tribe villages and Phuphing Palace, a favourite cool-season retreat for the royal family. The park is an important water catchment area, feeding streams that tumble over waterfalls, where they provide attractive picnic and camp-sites. A comprehensive survey of the park's flora, carried out by J. F. Maxwell at Chiang Mai University, has recorded at least 2,241 species of vascular plants. The park's diverse fauna includes at least 326 bird species, 500 butterflies, 300 moths, 61 mammals, 28 amphibians and 50 reptiles, all in a national park that covers just 261 square kilometres (101 square miles).

Deciduous Forests

For naturalists, the main interest of Doi Suthep is its diversity of forest types and birds. A walk on the mountain provides visitors with the most accessible introduction to the forest types of northern Thailand. The lower slopes are covered in deciduous dipterocarp-oak forest, composed of widely spaced trees: an abundance of *Shorea* and *Dipterocarpus* species, mingled with oaks,

Opposite, left above: Monthatharn Waterfall provides pleasant picnic sites and the opportunity for a cooling dip.

Opposite, left below: The Little Pied Flycatcher is a very common resident in Doi Suthep's evergreen forest.
Opposite, right: A monk plants a tree to restore forest to a degraded area.

Above, right: At the end of the rainy season many ginger species produce brightly coloured infructescences.

Map labels: To Mae Hong Son; 107; 1095; Mae Malai; THAILAND; Bangkok; 1001; Mae Rim; 1096; To Samoeng; Doi Suthep-Pui National Park; Doi Pui; Doi Suthep; Monthatharn Waterfall; Phuphing Palace; Huay Kaew Waterfall; Park Headquarters; 107; CHIANG MAI; Sisangwan Waterfall; 1269; Airport; 108; To Chom Thong; N

Right: *Common Barking Deer are the largest mammals remaining in the national park. Illegal hunters continue to shoot these beautiful animals, especially during the cool season.*

Right: *Doi Suthep is the home of many ancient spirits, some of which are thought to protect Chiang Mai from harm. Offerings to the spirits take many forms.*

Tristaniopsis burmanica, Anneslea fragrans, Craibiodendron stellatum, and so on. At the onset of the hot dry season, these trees produce a flaming red or orange canopy before they to drop their leaves in response to declining soil moisture. Many tree species flower when leafless, supposedly to make their flowers more visible to prospective pollinators. Flowering epiphytic orchids add colour to the canopy at the same time.

Deciduous dipterocarp-oak forest supports a wide range of birds, including Scarlet-backed Flowerpecker, Little Pied Flycatcher, Lineated Barbet and at least six different species of bulbul. Buzzards and other raptors commonly soar overhead, seeking prey such as Indochinese Ground Squirrels.

One of the most interesting mammals in this habitat is the Burmese Ferret-badger, still quite common on Doi Suthep. This nocturnal mammal has the black-and-white coloration of a badger with a body shape similar to that of a ferret. When threatened, it defends itself like a skunk, by spraying a foetid secretion from a gland near its anus into the face of its approaching enemy.

Mixed Deciduous Forest

Mixed deciduous forest, characterized by enormous *Dipterocarpus costatus* trees, which look like gigantic sticks of broccoli, begins to occur at an elevation of approximately 700 metres (2,300 feet). The trees are generally taller – up to 30 metres (98 feet) – than those of deciduous dipterocarp-oak forest, and the canopy is more-or-less closed. Many trees in this forest have beautiful flowers, which are particularly abundant in the late dry season (e.g. *Bauhinia variegata*, *Metadina trichotoma*). Amongst the ground flora, the aroid *Amorphophallus sootepensis* is one of more than 500 plant species named from specimens first collected on Doi Suthep, making the park of crucial significance to the science of plant taxonomy in Thailand.

Evergreen Forest

At an elevation of approximately 1,000 metres (3,281 feet), evergreen forest begins to dominate. On Doi Suthep this contains a very wide range of tree species. Beneath the dense canopy, light is in short supply and

Below: *A monk 'ordains' a tree by wrapping a robe around it. Trees often have high spiritual significance in Thai culture, and are believed to house spirits, both good and evil.*

some plants have evolved the means to do without it. Parasitic plants such as *Balanophora* (four species on Doi Suthep) and the striking, red *Sapria himalayana* extract nutriment from the roots of other plants, whilst delicate herbs such as *Hypopithys lanuginosa* feed on decomposing organic matter.

Doi Suthep's evergreen forest provides an important stopover for birds during their annual migrations. Common winter visitors include Grey Nightjar, Slender-billed Oriole and Orange-flanked Bush-robin (known in Europe as Red-flanked Bluetail). Some of Doi Suthep's more colourful evergreen forest residents include iridescent green pigeons, barbets and leafbirds, orange or yellow minivets and blue flycatchers and pittas.

Birds are not the only flying animals in the evergreen forest on Doi Suthep. Tiny grey squirrels avoid predators on the ground by gliding between trees using membranes stretched between their fore and hind legs. Flying lizards also occur. The upper slopes are also home to at least seven non-flying squirrel species and it is a last refuge for Doi Suthep's remaining larger mammals, including Common Palm Civet, Leopard Cat, Bush-tailed Porcupine and Common Barking Deer.

Forest Restoration

Like many of Thailand's national parks, Doi Suthep has suffered considerably from deforestation. Various estimates of forest cover range from only 40 per cent up to 70 per cent of the park. To help solve the problem of deforestation, one project is developing ways to restore forest to degraded areas. The Forest Restoration Research Unit (FORRU) is a joint initiative between the national park authority and Chiang Mai University's (CMU) Department of Biology. At an experimental tree nursery near the national park headquarters, FORRU staff and CMU students have developed new methods to propagate a wide range of forest tree species indigenous to the park. So far, more than 400 species have been germinated from seed and grown in the nursery. FORRU also helped to establish a community tree nursery at one of the Hmong villages in the national park, Ban Mae Sa Mai, where the feasibility of new tree-propagation methods developed by the project are tested by local people. In experimental plots near the village, FORRU is testing the suitability of the framework species method of forest restoration by planting mixtures of up to 30 tree species, capable of rapidly shading out weeds and attracting wildlife. Previously blamed for forest destruction, hill-tribe villagers in the park now join in tree-planting events and protect the planted trees from forest fire. With changing attitudes and greater scientific knowledge, the forest and its wildlife are slowly returning.

Spiritual Significance

In addition to its ecological value, Doi Suthep is of great spiritual significance to Chiang Mai's inhabitants. Doi Suthep's cultural history stretches much farther back than the founding of Wat Pratat. The Guardian Spirits of Chiang Mai reside on the mountain's lower slopes. Every year these spirits are placated in a ceremony that has its origins in myths that stretch back more than 1,000 years. The ceremony involves the sacrificial slaughter of a young buffalo, to satisfy the spirits' lust for meat. A medium then becomes possessed with the spirits and eats the raw buffalo carcass.

Right: *Folded hills disappear into the haze. A typical view of the northern highlands.*

Below: *The Leopard Cat, one of a few large mammals still surviving on Doi Suthep, is more tolerant of human disturbance than any other wild cat species, and is often found around villages.*

Nam Nao National Park

Elephants and Pine Trees

Easy forest walks and chances to see Asian Elephants and other large mammals in the unlikely setting of pine forest are the main attractions of this superb national park. Declared in 1972, Nam Nao National Park covers a total area of 990 square kilometres (386 square miles), but the value of the park is enormously enhanced by it being contiguous with the much larger Phu Kiew Wildlife Sanctuary to the south. In combination, the park and sanctuary protect a total of 2,550 square kilometres (984 square miles) of sandstone hills in the Phetchabun Range, mostly covered in deciduous dipterocarp forest and pine-dipterocarp forest, with narrow strips of evergreen forest bordering streams and rivers. The highest point in the park, the summit of Phu Phaa Jit, is at 1,271 metres (4,170 feet) above sea level.

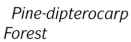

Pine-dipterocarp Forest

South of the national park headquarters and the main highway, an extensive network of tracks and trails meanders through one of the most extensive areas of open pine-dipterocarp forest in Thailand. Massive, three-needled pine trees (*Pinus kesiya*) tower above typical deciduous dipterocarp forest trees, which include several species of *Dipterocarpus*, *Shorea*, *Quercus* and *Dalbergia*, as well as *Ochna integerrima*, *Buchanania lanzan*, *Craibiodendron stellatum* and *Gluta usitata*.

Grasses and sedges dominate the ground flora, with splashes of colour provided by pink or white *Curcuma* species, yellow *Globba obscura* and the fragile pink orchid, *Arundina graminifolia*. *Aeginetia pedunculata* is a parasite on the roots of grasses. Its stalkless, purple-and-yellow, trumpet-shaped flowers appear just above the soil surface, particularly where fire has recently cleared away the surrounding vegetation. Also associated with pine trees is the curiously shaped fungus,

Opposite, above: Nam Nao National Park retains a small population of Asian Elephants, most easily seen lumbering through pine forests south of the park headquarters.

Opposite, below left: The Black-throated Laughingthrush is a common resident of Nam Nao National Park.

Opposite, below centre: Several caves within the park contain impressive formations. They are home to hundreds of thousands of bats.

Opposite, below right: Flowering orchids attract plant enthusiasts to Nam Nao's deciduous forest late in the dry season.

Above, right: Thaumantis diores sips rainwater running down a tree trunk.

Map labels:
THAILAND — Bangkok
Nam Nao National Park
Pha Hong
Park Headquarters
12
Ban Peak ▲
Sai Ngun Waterfall
Sai Thong Waterfall
Heo Sai Waterfall
Phu Phaa Jit ▲ 1271m (4170ft)
Suan Son ▲
Chulabhorn Reservoir
N

Macrolepida procera. The immature mushroom looks like a fluffy golf ball on the end of a thick, brown stalk, before the cap expands to the size of a dinner plate.

Large Mammals

Fires sweep across this area annually, but the sweet young grass, which shoots up afterwards, provides irresistible grazing for Banteng, Gaur, Sambar Deer, Common Barking Deer and Fea's Barking Deer. The latter, recognized by the IUCN as an endangered species, is mostly confined to the west of central Thailand and adjoining areas of Myanmar. It is distinguished from the Common Barking Deer by having a black dorsal surface to its tail (as opposed to brown on the Common Barking Deer). It is the Asian Elephants, however, that are the star attractions of this savannah-like area.

Approximately 100 are estimated to reside in the park. Being a semi-open habitat, it is probably easier to see elephants here during the daytime than it is at Khao Yai. Lumbering through the pine trees in small herds, they create an almost surrealistic vision.

National park staff have created a series of small ponds and salt licks scattered across this area, which act like a magnet for wildlife, especially during the evenings. Wildlife watchers keeping vigil at these spots at dawn or dusk will rarely be disappointed. The pools and salt licks draw not only herbivores and wildlife enthusiasts, however: there are also an estimated 20 to 50 Tigers in the park that doubtless stalk prey attracted by the water and minerals. In addition to Tigers, Clouded Leopard and the elusive and highly endangered Marbled Cat have been recorded.

Below: *Sambar are Thailand's largest deer species. They require large amounts of calcium to replace their antlers each year and can often be seen at mineral licks.*

Other Wildlife

Nam Nao and Phu Kiew were probably the last strong-holds of the Sumatran Rhino and Eld's Deer in Thailand, but it is very unlikely that either of these two species still exists in the wild. Plenty of other species are, however, still present in the park, including three species of macaque monkey (Pig-tailed, Long-tailed and Stump-tailed) and White-handed Gibbons. Both bear species (Asiatic Black and Malayan Sun), as well as Asian Wild Dog, Yellow-throated Marten and Crestless Himalayan Porcupine, are reportedly present.

One of the best places for watching birds is along the network of short nature trails around the park head-quarters, which showcase the full range of forest types within the park. Confirmed bird species for Nam Nao number 252. Notable species include Mountain Hawk Eagle, Eurasian Hobby, Silver Pheasant, Coral-billed Ground Cuckoo, Rufous-tailed Robin, Siberian Rubythroat and Verditer Flycatcher.

The park also has quite a reputation amongst but-terfly enthusiasts. Some of the more colourful species include Common Birdwing, Paris Peacock, Banded Swallowtail, Common Blue Bottle, Red Lacewing, Lurcher and Great Nawab.

Left: *With its dense heads of greenish-yellow flowers and thorny stems,* Trevesia palmata *is unmistakable. It is a small tree found in the understorey of ever-green forests.*

Above: *The Verditer Flycatcher can be seen swooping on flying insects from exposed perches, especially along the edge of the forest.*

Left: *The Green Pit-viper stalks its prey in the forest canopy at night. It is a highly poisonous snake and should be given a wide berth if seen.*

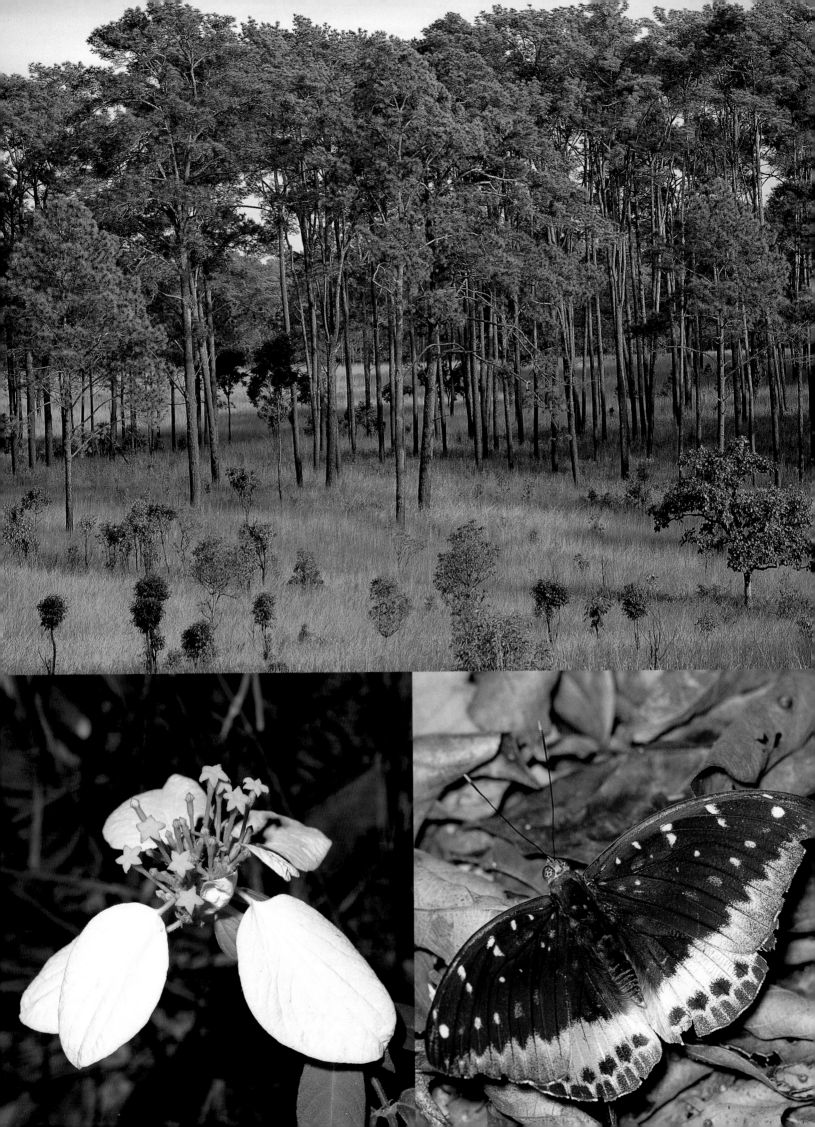

THUNG SALAENG LUANG NATIONAL PARK

Flower Meadows and a Refuge for Rebels

Established in 1963 as Thailand's third national park, Thung Salaeng Luang protects 1,262 square kilometres (487 square miles) of forested mountains, reaching a maximum elevation of 1,028 metres (3,372 feet), as well as attractive flower meadows, in Thailand's lower northern region.

Kaeng Sopa Waterfalls

The scenic highlight of the park is Kaeng Sopa Waterfalls, near Km 71 on Highway 12. In a country where the attractiveness of waterfalls tends

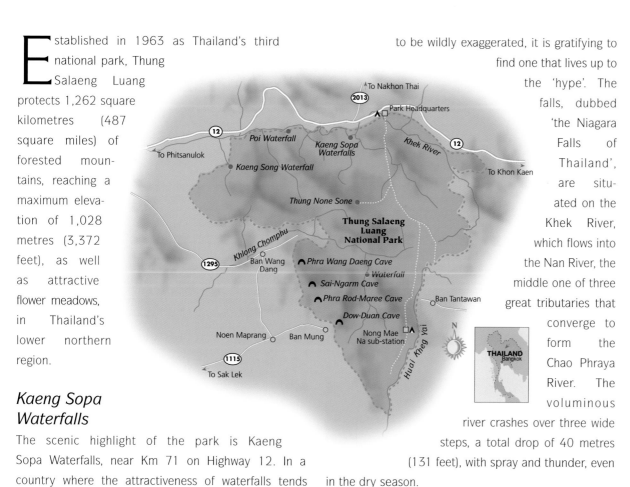

to be wildly exaggerated, it is gratifying to find one that lives up to the 'hype'. The falls, dubbed 'the Niagara Falls of Thailand', are situated on the Khek River, which flows into the Nan River, the middle one of three great tributaries that converge to form the Chao Phraya River. The voluminous river crashes over three wide steps, a total drop of 40 metres (131 feet), with spray and thunder, even in the dry season.

The Meadows

Although most of the park is covered by deciduous dipterocarp and mixed evergreen-deciduous forest, it is the open pine savannahs (*thung* in Thai), occupying a mere two per cent of the park's area, that are the central feature. They support varied communities of wildflowers and provide grazing for wildlife. Frequent fires, shallow soils and seasonal drought maintain these grasslands. Thung Salaeng Luang, which lends its name to the national park, is itself named after a small, fire-resistant tree species, *Strychnos nux-vomica*, which is common on the grassland. The seeds of this tree contain strychnine,

Opposite, above: *Open grasslands (thung in Thai) studded with pine trees are the main features at Thung Salaeng Luang.*

Opposite, below left: Mussaenda parva, *a common and widespread shrub in both deciduous and evergreen forest types, flowers in the cool, dry season.*

Opposite, below right: *Thung Salaeng Luang is famous for its butterflies. This species is* Euthalia pardalis.

Above, right: Ardesia crenata, *an evergreen treelet, produces edible fruits relished by birds and mammals from August to February.*

Location: In provinces of Phitsanulok and Phetchabun, 60 km (37 miles) east of Phitsanulok.

Climate: Monsoonal; mean annual rainfall 1,200-2,000 mm (47-78 in); mean annual temperature approximately 27°C (81°F); rainy season May–October; cool, dry season November–January; hot, dry season February–April (mean monthly temperature over 30°C/86°F).

When to Go: October to February, best for wild flowers, waterfalls and large mammals.

Access: The park headquarters reached by travelling 79 km (49 miles) east along Highway 12, from Phitsanulok. Public buses between Phitsanulok and Khon Kaen stop near Kaeng Sopa Falls and park headquarters.

Permits: Fees at waterfalls.

Equipment: Insect repellent; strong shoes and light clothes for forest walks; a torch for caves; waterproof gear.

Facilities: Bungalows for rent at park headquarters and Nong Mae Na substation; several campsites; visitor centre with small exhibition at park headquarters; resorts and restaurants along Highway 12; nature trails and long treks with guides. Visitors should keep to marked paths, because of landmines.

Wildlife: Excellent birdwatching, butterfly spotting and botanizing.

Visitor Activities: Forest walks; visiting waterfalls and caves; birdwatching.

Right: Livistona *palms can
still sometimes be seen in
evergreen forest along
streams and rivers, but they
are under considerable
pressure from the
horticultural trade.*

*Below: Rather extravagantly
dubbed the 'Niagara Falls'
of Thailand, the magnificent
Kaeng Sopa Waterfalls are
one of the scenic highlights
of the national park.*

one of the world's most powerful nerve toxins. Another botanical feature of this area is the parasitic plant *Christisonia siamensis*, a species endemic to Thailand, which feeds on grass roots. Its white tubular flowers, rimmed with dark purple-and-yellow spots, appear to sit directly on the soil surface.

A trek of 20 kilometres (12½ miles) through evergreen forest leads to Thung None Sone, at the heart of the national park, a beautiful savannah studded with pine trees and *Phoenix* palms. These palms rise from the ashes of the fires that sweep across the savannah every dry season. Their growing points are insulated against the flames by being sunken within the woody stem of the plant and surrounded by dead leaf stalks. After fire, new green leaves sprout from the blackened plant. Colourful herbs, such as the purple *Barleria strigosa* and *Pseuderanthemum andersonii*, insect-eating pitcher plants, ground orchids and gingers also provide interest for botanists.

Small mammals include Yellow-throated Marten, Masked Palm Civet, Black Giant Squirrel, Long-tailed Macaque and Dusky Langur. White-handed Gibbons can still be found in more remote areas of the park, but their population has recently crashed to just a handful of individuals.

A total of 203 bird species have been confirmed within the national park, including several rare birds of prey such as Mountain Hawk Eagle, White-rumped Falcon and Peregrine Falcon. Other interesting bird species include Great Hornbill, Great Slaty Woodpecker, Coral-billed Ground Cuckoo and Silver-breasted Broadbill.

The Sad Story of Schombugk's Deer

Thung Salaeng Luang may have been the last stronghold of Schombugk's Deer, a species endemic to Thailand. It became extinct in the 1930s, the only deer species to have disappeared since the Stone Age. With large, splayed hooves and spreading antlers, this deer species lived on open swampy plains and grasslands, avoiding

Left: *Some of the meadows in Thung Salaeng Luang National Park are studded with* Phoenix loureiri *Palms, named after their ability to regrow rapidly after fire. The fruits are edible.*

Below: *The open meadows of Thung Salaeng Luang National Park provide almost perfect conditions for spotting large mammals, such as wild cattle, deer and occasionally elephants.*

Fauna

The open grasslands and savannahs of Thung Salaeng Luang provide excellent grazing for the park's large herbivores, and good opportunities for wildlife enthusiasts to view these animals in fairly open conditions. At dusk, Common Barking Deer, Sambar Deer and the occasional Gaur emerge from the surrounding forest to graze on the meadows, whilst Common Wild Pigs root around for corms and tubers. Siamese Hares are abundant and can often be seen in the daytime. Such animals provide prey for Asian Wild Dogs and perhaps the occasional Tiger. Although no one has seen a Tiger for quite some time, Tiger tracks are still reported by park rangers. A small herd of Asian Elephants is resident within the park and has increased its numbers from about 20 in the 1980s to about 30 today. The park authority is establishing new salt licks to encourage Asian Elephants and other large mammals not to migrate outside the park and cause conflict with surrounding farmers.

dense forests, which restricted its movement. It was fairly common in open areas at Thung Salaeng Luang until the 1920s. The last reported wild Schombugk's Deer was shot in 1932 in Kanchanaburi Province. Monks at a temple in Samut Sakorn cared for a free-ranging tame male, possibly the last of its kind, as late as 1938, but a drunkard, who mistook it for a wild deer, clubbed it to death.

Other Attractions

Along the western boundary of the park are four limestone caves, which make interesting destinations for long-distance hikers. Butterflies are also an attraction. The area around Wang Nam Yen rapids is said to be especially rewarding for butterfly watchers. Thung Salaeng Luang was a stronghold of Communist insurgents from the late 1960s to the early 1980s. The deciding battles between Communist and Government forces took place at Khao Khor to the east of the park, where the Communists were finally defeated in 1982. Part of a Communist settlement and rice fields have, however, been preserved in the southeast of the park and are now features on an excellent nature trail, which starts at the Nong Mae Na substation. Landmines from this period are still occasionally unearthed in the park, so walkers should not stray from the paths.

Right: *Streams like this become an important refuge for wildlife during the dry season. Forests by streams usually support more species than dry forests and are very important for the conservation of biodiversity.*

Opposite: *The Black Giant Squirrel feeds on fruits and seeds in the treetops, rarely venturing to the ground. It is capable of leaping long distances between trees.*

KHAO YAI NATIONAL PARK

Thailand's Premier Tropical Forest Park

Created in September 1962, Thailand's first national park, Khao Yai, protects a large remnant (2,168 square kilometres/836 square miles) of a vast forest, which once covered most of northeastern Thailand. Most of the forest was cleared to make way for rapid agricultural development after the Second World War and for road building during the Vietnamese War, but thanks to the tireless campaigning of Thailand's foremost naturalist, the late Dr Boonsong Lekagul, Khao Yai was saved from destruction. It now appears on satellite images as an isolated island of forest in a sea of agricultural land.

Khao Yai retains excellent forest and wildlife and

Opposite, above: *This campsite affords a rare sideways view of the forest structure at Khao Yai.*

Opposite, below left: *Silver Pheasants can be seen in evergreen forest around the park headquarters.*

Opposite, below right: *The Pileated Gibbon is one of Thailand's many endangered species.*

Above, right: Urena lobata *is a common weedy herb found throughout Isaan in disturbed areas.*

Previous pages:
Page 110: *An open grassland in Phu Kiew Wildlife Sanctuary.* Page 111: *Gibbon calls are perhaps the most evocative sound of Thailand's forests.*

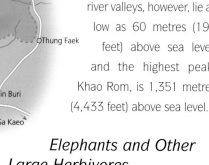

provides the most accessible location for eco-tourists to view large mammals in Thailand. It plays host to 71 mammal species (including at least 16 bats), more than one-third of Thailand's bird species (at least 340), at least 189 butterflies and an estimated 2,500 vascular plant species.

A large part of the park is a rolling plateau of sandstone, ranging in elevation from 600 to 1,000 metres (1,968–3,281 feet). Some of the river valleys, however, lie as low as 60 metres (197 feet) above sea level, and the highest peak, Khao Rom, is 1,351 metres (4,433 feet) above sea level.

Elephants and Other Large Herbivores

The park is mostly covered by dense, primary, evergreen forest, with small areas of open grassland, the result of cultivation by villagers and bandits, long since evicted from the park, and an abandoned golf course. Although 'unnatural', these areas provide essential grazing for the park's large herbivores and give visitors excellent opportunities to view wildlife. Deer can sometimes be seen grazing in the open in broad daylight, but it is during the evening that these grasslands come alive with Asian Elephants, Sambar Deer, Common Barking Deer, Common Wild Pigs and Gaurs. Wildlife is easily seen from the road or from wildlife observation towers.

Khao Yai is undoubtedly the best site in Thailand to see Asian Elephants in their natural habitat. It is estimated that 140–200 elephants live in the park. Their footprints and dung can be seen everywhere. Elephants

Above: The White-handed Gibbon exists in two colour variations; a light form and a dark one, shown here. Pairings usually occur between individuals of the same colour form. Genes for the dark fur are dominant over those for light fur.

Above, right: The light colour form of the White-handed Gibbon. It's disproportionately long arms and strong grasping hands enable it to swing with ease from branch to branch, a form of locomotion known as brachiation.

are particularly common along the road, which bisects the park, between Km 25 and Km 35. Several salt licks in this area attract not only elephants but also many other animals, best observed at dawn or dusk. To view nocturnal wildlife, the park headquarters organizes 'spotlight safaris'. Visitors are driven around the park at night in trucks mounted with powerful lamps and are almost guaranteed sightings of deer, Asian Elephants, giant flying squirrels, civets, porcupines, bats and many other species.

Reports of up to 50 Tigers living in the park continue to circulate, but recent surveys indicate that very few Tigers survive there. Other cats present include Leopard, Leopard Cat, Clouded Leopard and the highly endangered Marbled Cat, but sightings of all these species are exceedingly rare.

Gibbons

Khao Yai is the only place where two of Thailand's gibbon species, the White-handed and the Pileated, come into contact. The White-handed Gibbon is distributed from Sumatra through Malaysia to northern Thailand, Yunnan and parts of Laos. This species has two colour forms,

either light tan, or dark brown to black, and is distinguished by a white ring completely surrounding the facial features. Pileated Gibbons, restricted to eastern Thailand, Laos and Cambodia, are sexually dimorphic. Mature males are black, whilst mature females are buff with a black crown, throat and chest. The two species have different songs. White-handed Gibbons rouse campers with soaring, melodious whoops, whereas the song of the Pileated Gibbon is similar to the beat of a drum. Although rare, interbreeding between the species does sometimes occur, with the hybrid offspring singing an intermediate song. Khao Yai is home to the longest continuous study of gibbons in the world. Teams from Mahidol University (led by Dr Warren Brockelman) and from the Max Plank Institute for Biological Anthropology (led by Dr Ulrich Reichard) have been observing gibbon family life and studying their habitat needs there for more than 20 years.

Other primates in the park include the Slow Loris and Pig-tailed Macaques; the latter roam around the park in large troops. Asian Wild Dogs can occasionally be seen hunting deer in packs. Both the Asiatic Black Bear and Malayan Sunbear also occur.

Left: Massive emergent trees soar above the main canopy of the evergreen forest that is characteristic of Khao Yai.

Below, left: A signboard in the Khao Yai National Park alerts visitors to the presence of Tigers.

Below: Although Thailand's Tiger population has been much reduced in recent years, a few still remain in Khao Yai, particularly around the park headquarters.

Hornbills

Khao Yai is an important research site for hornbills. Dr Pilai Poonswad and her team from Mahidol University have been conducting long-term studies on the diet and breeding ecology of hornbills in Khao Yai since the early 1980s. Four species live in the park: Wreathed, Brown, Oriental Pied and Great. Hornbills are primarily frugivorous, with figs comprising a large part of their diet, but they can also take insects and small reptiles, especially during the breeding season. They survive only in undisturbed forest with large trees, since they nest in large holes in tree trunks. The females seal themselves inside the nesting cavity, blocking the entrance with faeces and other materials, leaving only a narrow slit, through which the male passes food. Females begin their imprisonment in January to March and the chicks usually fledge in May or June. Outside the breeding season, Wreathed Hornbills provide Khao Yai's most impressive bird spectacle, as they start to congregate together in flocks, small at first but gradually increasing to contain up to 1,000 individuals. They come together to feed and roost in the largest forest trees.

Below: *The Great Hornbill is Thailand's largest hornbill species. Its huge bill and wide gape enable it to disperse the largest of tree seeds.*

In addition to hornbills, the park boasts an impressive array of rare birds of prey, including Peregrine Falcon, Mountain Hawk Eagle, Rufous-bellied Eagle, Grey-headed Fish-eagle and Buffy Fish-owl. Among the park's other notable birds are Narcissus Flycatcher, Silver Oriole, Coral-billed Ground Cuckoo, Oriental Cuckoo, Yellow-footed Pigeon, Silver Pheasant, Siamese Fireback, Blue and Eared Pittas, Orange-breasted and Red-headed Trogons and four species of broadbill.

Activities and Attractions

Wildlife watching is by far the most popular activity in Khao Yai, usually undertaken by hiking along the myriad of well-marked trails which radiate out from the park headquarters, ranging in length from 1.5–8 kilometres (1–5 miles). In addition, several waterfalls are well worth a visit, the tallest and most spectacular of which is Haew Narok, which plummets 80 metres (262 feet) in two huge leaps. Haew Suwat is another popular waterfall on the upper reaches of the Lam Takhong River. The rivers provide opportunities for white-water rafting along the park's southeastern boundary. Exhilarating trips of up to three hours can be arranged. Mountain biking is also being promoted in the park; bicycles can be rented from the national park headquarters. Advised routes take cyclists past most of the wildlife viewing points around the centre of the park.

Above: *Large troops of Pig-tailed Macaques, with up to 40 individuals, roam widely throughout the park.*

Below, left: *The Siamese Fireback can be seen in evergreen forest around the national park headquarters.*

Below: *The white ear patch shows that this Red Jungle-fowl belongs to the eastern subspecies. It is a close relative of the domestic chicken.*

Ao Phangnga Marine National Park & Krabi

Dramatic Karst Scenery

A highly fragmented spine of limestone runs down the western side of Thailand. This limestone formed during the Permian Period, 225–280 million years ago, as shellfish and corals accumulated in a shallow sea along a barrier reef that stretched from southern China to Borneo. For millions of years, the limestone was buried and compressed beneath younger sediments, but 3–60 million years ago India collided with the rest of Asia, thrusting up the Himalayas as well as a tail of lower hills running down Thailand's western border with Myanmar. The long-buried layers of Permian limestone were fractured and exposed, then eroded by monsoonal rains. Plant roots cracked open the rock, and acid from decomposing humus dissolved

Opposite: *Towering limestone cliffs, densely clad in luxuriant vegetation and eroded by wind and waves into extraordinary formations, are the dominant scenic features.*

Above, right: *Surgeonfish are so-named because they bear sharp spines on either side of the tail, which may be used to inflict wounds on enemies.*

the limestone, widening the cracks. Water, seeping through the fractured rock, formed underground streams and vast cave systems. Along the coast, fluctuating sea levelsand wave movement sculptured the limestone into a bewildering array of formations. This breathtaking seascape is termed drowned karstland by geologists and reaches its zenith in Phangnga Bay.

Ao Phangnga Marine National Park

Phangnga Bay presents a landscape of immense limestone crags, set amidst mangrove forest in a shallow sea, which is barely one metre deep in places. The bay was declared a marine national park in 1981. It covers 40 sculptured islands, totalling 53 square kilometres (20 square miles), and 347 square kilometres (134 square miles) of cloudy, turquoise ocean. The craggy cliffs, rising to a height of up to 400 metres (1,312 feet), are often pockmarked with gaping cave entrances. Rock paintings, dating back at least 3,000 years, that depict crocodiles, dolphins, sharks and people have been found at Khao Khian, near the mouth of the Phangnga River.

Location: The western and southern coastline between the provincial capitals of Krabi and Phangnga Provinces.

Climate: Average annual temperature 23°C (73°F); average annual rainfall 2,380 mm (94 in); hottest in May–April; coolest in November–February; rainy season May–October.

When to Go: Phangnga Bay is sheltered and calm all year around, but the best time to visit is November to May.

Access: By organized tours or rented cars and boats from the tourism centres of Krabi and Phuket. Thai Airways flies to both Phuket and Krabi.

Permits: None required.

Equipment: Protection against the sun is essential when travelling by boat; insect repellent; snorkelling or scuba gear; rock-climbing equipment.

Facilities: A wide range of accommodation and restaurants in the town of Krabi, the resort beaches of Phuket and at Laem Phra Nang; simple guesthouses in the town of Phangnga; Forest Department bungalows at Phangnga and Had Nopparat Thara; organized tours and boats for charter from Krabi and Phuket resort beaches.

Wildlife: Monkeys, flying foxes, seabirds, dolphins.

Visitor Activities: Birdwatching; boat trips and sea canoeing; visiting caves; rock climbing; snorkelling and scuba diving.

Sea Canoes

Most tourist boats head straight for 'James Bond Island', the famous setting for the film, *The Man with the Golden Gun*. Another busy attraction is the so-called 'Sea Gypsy Village' (the community is actually Muslim, not Sea Gypsy), comprising approximately 500 houses on stilts around Koh Panyi. A gentler way to see the national park, however, is to book a trip with one of many tour companies now offering travel by sea canoe. Canoes allow access to partially submerged cave passages and massive, hidden, collapsed caverns, known as *hongs*, inside the islands. Some *hongs* contain secret lagoons, whilst others support tiny patches of forest.

The water is too turbid to support corals. A few Dugongs may still occur in the marine park and dolphins are sometimes seen. At least 96 bird species have been recorded, including several rare or endangered species such as Malaysian Plover, Asian Dowitcher, Buffy Fish-owl and Dark-throated Oriole. Amongst the trees that cling to the cliff faces, Common Flying Foxes roost, setting forth at dusk to forage for fruit. Amongst the mangroves, Smooth Indian Otters chase fish, whilst the carnivorous frog *Rana cancrivora* feasts on fiddler crabs.

Plants

Plants that gain a tenuous roothold in the cracks and crevices of the limestone crags face a difficult life. They are exposed to extreme temperature fluctuations and

Above: *Although Railay Beach is situated on the mainland, it is accessible only by boat from Krabi town. It is widely regarded as one of the most beautiful beaches in the world.*

Right: *Growing up to 35 centimetres (14 inches) across, the Blue Sea Star (Linkia laevigata) is a common inhabitant of Andaman Sea reefs.*

the full force of monsoonal deluges but, as soon as the rain stops, water rapidly drains away through cracks in the rock, leaving the plants in almost continuous drought conditions. With heat reflected from the light-coloured rock, daytime temperatures soar, threatening plants with desiccation.

However, fortunately many plant species have evolved the means to conserve water and survive in these harsh conditions, including the cycad *Cycas rumphii*, a relic from the age of dinosaurs, with its tough palm-like leaves, deep roots and convoluted woody stem, capable of storing large quantities of water. The palm *Maxburretia furtadiana*, recently discovered by botanists, is endemic to the limestone karst of southern Thailand. With beautiful, fan-shaped leaves, this unique palm can grow to a height of up to 5 metres (16 feet), and roots directly into cracks in the limestone.

Krabi

Approximately 90 kilometres (56 miles) south of Phangnga, Krabi is a charming fishing town, which takes its name from an ancient, legendary sword, or *krabi*, purportedly discovered nearby. Mangroves in the Krabi River estuary provide interesting boat trips for bird-watchers. Mangrove Pitta, Masked Finfoot, Mangrove Blue Flycatcher, Nordmann's Greenshank and five species of kingfisher are just some of the many birds that can be seen.

Above: *The Hill Myna can be seen in forests throughout Thailand. It has the ability to mimic the human voice and for this reason is often kept in captivity.*

Left: *Many tour companies in Krabi now offer sea canoeing as a more ecologically friendly alternative to conventional boat tours for exploring the mangroves and caves.*

Above: *The dominant geological feature of the Krabi–Phangnga coastline is what geologists call drowned karstland; dramatic pinnacles of limestone plunging into an azure sea.*

Above, right: *These fantastic limestone formations are formed by the constant percolation of rainwater through the limestone and fluctuating sea levels over many thousands of years.*

Opposite: *Long-tailed Macaques, one of six primate species confirmed present in Ao Phangnga Marine National Park. Grooming serves the practical function of removing irritating parasites from the fur.*

The main attractions of Krabi are reached by boat from the town's main pier. Laem Phra Nang (the mainland part of Had Nopparat Thara–Mu Ko Phi Phi Marine National Park) is a limestone headland so rugged that it is completely inaccessible by road. Awesome, sheer cliffs 250 metres (820 feet) high provide a dramatic backdrop to the beaches of Railay and Phra Nang, ranked amongst the five most beautiful in the world. Enclosed and sunken in the heart of the cave is the remarkable Princess Pool, a classic marine *hong*, which fills with seawater, via an underground passage at high tide.

Long-tailed Macaques, one of the most visible mammals on limestone karst, are common around Laem Phra Nang. On forested crags, these monkeys eat small animals and fruits, especially figs that readily root in limestone cracks, whilst down by the sea they forage for crabs and other marine animals.

Caves are prominent features of karstland. Not only are the caves of Krabi richly adorned with stalagmites and stalactites, but several also contain archaeological evidence of the earliest human beings to live in Thailand. Stone tools and hearths, belonging to the ancient Hoabinhians, dated at 43,000 years old, were found a few kilometres north of Krabi town in 1982. Younger,

Stone Age cave paintings, tools, jewellery and human remains have been found in several other caves, particularly in and around Thaan Bok Koranee National Park, 42 kilometres (26 miles) north of the town of Krabi. Established in 1998, this 104-square kilometre (40-square-mile) national park includes nine caves, several accessible only by boat, and a botanical garden. Small waterfalls, cascading into emerald-green pools, create a fairy-tale landscape which attracts hundreds of picnickers at weekends.

Rock Climbing

The area around Krabi and Phangnga is fast becoming one of Southeast Asia's premier rock-climbing sites. A tourist magazine recently described it thus '...for the world's rock climbers, Krabi is not just a Mecca; for them, it's as if the cornucopia of routes on offer up the many sheer walls rising up out of Phangnga Bay and around mean they've died and gone to mountaineering heaven.' Since the mid-1990s there has been a phenomenal increase in this sport, particularly around Laem Phra Nang, where 300 climbing routes have been pioneered. Any of the bungalow resorts at Laem Phra Nang can provide rock-climbing instructors and guides.

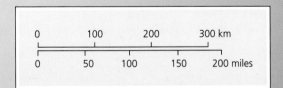

THE PHILIPPINES

The northern half of **Luzon**, the largest of the Philippines' islands, consists of two large plains and three major mountain ranges, including the Zambales Mountains. At the southern end of the mountain range, Subic Watershed Forest is one of Luzon's few remaining tracts of lowland dipterocarp rainforest and is one of the best places in the country to get close to wildlife.

Just south of Manila, **Mindoro** is a wild and rugged island, sparsely populated and relatively undeveloped. The majority of the population live along the coasts where some spectacular coral reefs can be found. The most easily visited are those at Puerto Galera, in the far north of the island.

The island of Sibuyan is dominated by Mount Guiting Guiting, and much of its natural environment, from coral reefs offshore to mossy forest and grassland around the mountain's peaks, is intact. Sibuyan's fauna and flora are distinct, having several unique species of mammal.

Similarly, the **eastern Visayas and Mindanao** also form a single major biogeographic zone. Much of the landscape is rugged, with the Kitanglad range and Mount Apo cutting across large parts of Mindanao. There are a number of large forest areas as yet unprotected by the country's new Integrated Protected Areas System (IPAS).

Lying to the west of the main body of the Philippines, **Palawan** consists of one main island and an estimated 1,768 smaller ones. Palawan is still relatively under-populated and wild, with forests covering two-thirds of the land and extensive coral reefs around its coasts.

Above: *The shore of Balicasag Island, surrounded by a dazzling white beach.*

95

SUBIC WATERSHED FOREST RESERVE

Lush Forests in an Old Naval Base

Situated 130 kilometres (80 miles) northwest of Manila and within the confines of what until 1992 was the USA's largest overseas naval base, the 10,000 hectare (24,700 acres) forest of Subic Bay is one of the Philippines' most accessible wilderness areas. Deliberately protected by the American military as a source of water, a security shield and for use in jungle survival training, the forest received a level of protection that could only be dreamed of for similar wilderness areas in the rest of the country.

When the navy pulled out the entire base and its 10,000 hectares (24,700) of forest became a special economic zone administered by the Subic Bay Metropolitan Authority (SBMA). Much of the base area has been turned into an industrial and commercial centre, but despite the obvious pressures this creates for nature conservation the Subic Watershed Forest Reserve remains one of the largest and healthiest surviving areas of lowland tropical rainforest in Luzon. It is contiguous with the forests of Bataan Natural Park,

Opposite: *Mangroves in Triboa Bay, in the NavMag area of Subic Bay. The pneumatophores, or aerial roots, that surround the mangroves enable the trees to 'breathe' even when immersed in water.*

Above right: *The Northern Shoveler is amongst hundreds of ducks that visit the Triboa Bay mangroves during winter.*

lying to the east and south, and these two areas – although still administered separately – have officially become part of the Subic-Bataan Natural Park, one of the country's 10 priority protected areas under the new IPAS programme.

Forests from Shore to Hill

Subic Bay is a large, deep inlet situated just north of Manila Bay, surrounded by hills, its mouth guarded by Grande Island. The topography along the eastern shore, where the economic zone is located, is quite gentle, backed by rolling hills. Most of the commercial and industrial area was cleared of trees long ago, but to the south the forest extends down to the edge of the airport, and encircles a number of residential areas, such as Cubi.

The main forested area lies still further south, however, in a region known as the Naval Magazine (today called simply NavMag), where there are still scores of underground bunkers once used to store ammunition. It is here that the forest cover reaches its most complete and impressive state, with mature stands of gigantic dipterocarp trees that stretch from the hills right down to the shore. Several of the small coves and river mouths are sites of extensive mangrove swamp, while the sandy shores are lined with beach forest, all of which merge with the dipterocarp forest immediately behind.

Location: 130 km (80 miles) northwest of Manila, on west coast of Luzon. Economic zone adjacent to town of Olongapo.

Climate: Tropical.Dry season November–May. Heaviest rain July–September. In hottest months (April–May) temperatures can reach 35°C (95°F). Coolest months January–February.

When to go: January–February.

Access: Cars can be hired in Manila. Frequent buses to Olongapo take about three hours. Flights from Manila's domestic airport.

Permits: Only for the NavMag; obtainable from the SBMA's Ecology Centre. Entire economic zone is duty-free so passports and identity checked whenever you enter or leave the zone.

Equipment: Walking shoes, light clothing, insect repellent, vehicle (especially if going into NavMag).

Facilities: International standard hotels within the Subic economic zone; cheaper places available in Olongapo. Public transport around the zone, but not into the NavMag. Excellent roads. Guides for trails around Pamulaklakin and JEST. Some trails also in NavMag.

Wildlife: Forest birds, including many endemics. Ducks in mangroves. Macaques common and monitor lizards seen occasionally. Sharks common in Triboa Bay. Colony of fruit bats .

Visitor Activities: Hiking, birdwatching, bat-watching, photography, jungle survival training. Diving on wrecks.

(Map labels) ZAMBALES · To Manila · N · Subic Bay · Olongapo · Subic Freeport · Olongapo Bay · Cubi Point · Subic International Airport · Pamulaklakin · Cubi · Jungle Environmental Survival Training Camp · Triboa Bay · Subic Watershed Forest Reserve · Naval Magazine (Nav Mag) · Binanga Bay · BATAAN · Luzon · Manila · Malaysia

Far right: *The White-bellied Sea-eagle, a fairly common raptor found right across Southeast Asia, is often seen soaring over Subic's coastline, hunting in the seas, but nesting and resting in the forest.*

Right: *Two species of fruit bat roost as a colony in a cluster of large trees during the daytime.*

Although the forest is extensive and often dense, in places the canopy is quite open, there being a large number of dead trees. These were killed in 1991 by ash fallout from the eruption of nearby Mount Pinatubo. The forest is rapidly regrowing, but while the canopy remains open birdwatching is considerably easier than it would be in a wholly closed-canopy forest!

Teeming with Wildlife

As a result of the protection, the forest's wildlife is intact and relatively tame. Forest birds are especially abundant, and many species such as Stork-billed Kingfisher, Sooty Woodpecker, Lesser Tree Swift, Dollarbird, Blue-throated Bee-eater and even Luzon Hornbills are all readily visible from the many roads that cut through the forest. The mangroves within the NavMag area, particularly in Triboa Bay, teem with ducks, especially during the winter months, when hundreds of Philippine Mallard (an endemic bird) and

Left: *The Golden-crowned Flying Fox, one of the world's largest fruit bats, is one of the two species that make up the Subic fruit bat colony.*

the migratory Tufted Duck and Northern Shoveler can be seen. White-bellied Sea-eagles, Philippine Serpent-eagles and Brahminy Kites are all frequently and easily seen soaring above the forest canopy.

Long-tailed Macaques are also ubiquitous, often sighted sitting and feeding in family groups on the roadsides. Fruit bats are easily seen since a large colony roosts in tall trees close to Cubi. The thousands of bats that exist here consist of a mixture of the Philippine Giant Fruit Bat and the Golden-crowned Flying Fox, two of the world's largest bats, with a wingspan of up to two metres (six feet). The latter is endemic to the Philippines and highly endangered, so this site is of major importance to conservation.

Offshore, there are coral reefs around Grande Island and along the bay's outermost shores, while sharks, such as Blacktip Reef Sharks, patrol the inshore waters, and both Green and Olive Ridley Turtles still nest on a number of the beaches, including those along the very perimeter of the airport.

People of the Forest

Despite living within a military base, a population of Negritos, known as Aeta in this part of Luzon, were allowed to continue their existence in the forest. Today about 100 families still live here. No longer practising a fully hunter-gatherer existence, but engaged in farming and some aspects of the commercial economy, for years these people trained American soldiers for jungle survival. Today, they offer their skills to civilians as part of the SBMA's ecotourism programme, and can act as forest guides.

Forest Ecotourism

Subic Bay offers the visitor one of the most rewarding opportunities in the Philippines for a close encounter with a true wilderness area. The bat roost is easily viewed from a hillside lookout point right in Cubi, while anyone wishing to learn about jungle survival can take a special course from the Jungle Environmental Survival Training Camp (JEST). The men here offer visitors anything from a two-hour forest hike, during which a whole host of plants are pointed out and their uses demonstrated, to a week-long course. Nearby at

Above right: *Some of the forest's biggest trees have huge buttress roots to support them in the shallow soil.*

Right: *Wild figs are plentiful in lowland rainforests such as Subic's and are a major food source for fruit bats.*

Above: *An Aeta tribesman living in the Subic forest demonstrates the traditional method of catching fish in the forest rivers.*

Right: *A member of JEST demonstrates how to make a rice steamer out of bamboo cut in the forest. All that is needed is the right knife.*

Pamulaklakin, the Aeta have established a model village where aspects of their traditional culture and lifestyle are demonstrated.

These three sites are outside the NavMag area and are easily accessible to the visitor. For trips into the NavMag it is necessary to obtain a permit from the SBMA's Ecology Centre and to have one of their forest rangers as a guide. A vehicle is also necessary, as public transport does not extend into the NavMag. In this region the main activity is hiking, and there are a variety of routes to be explored. Trails lead down to the mangroves of Triboa Bay, for example, or through the dipterocarp forest up to Hill 394, the highest point within the economic zone.

Opposite: *A Karpia tree, one of the giants of the lowland rainforest, but not a dipterocarp tree, towers through Subic's open canopy.*

PUERTO GALERA MARINE RESERVE

A Well-protected Submarine World

Puerto Galera is a well-known and beautiful beach resort area lying at the northern tip of Mindoro, about 130 kilometres (80 miles) south of Manila. Not only is it blessed with an almost uncountable number of beaches scattered among its many islands and bays, but beneath the waves are to be found some of the country's most stunning coral reefs. It is not surprising that this has become one of the Philippines' most popular attractions, with both overseas visitors and Filipinos coming to enjoy the beautiful scenery, both above and below the water.

UNESCO Protection for the Reefs

So extensive and diverse are these reefs that they have been the centre of scientific study for a good many years, the University of the Philippines establishing a marine

Opposite far left above: *Feeding fish is a popular activity for divers, though one that should not be recommended.*

Opposite far left middle: *Tubastraea cup corals, with their tentacles protruding as they 'hunt' for food in the current.*

Opposite far left below: *A Moray Eel makes a foray from a crevass in the reef.*

Opposite left: *A barrel sponge surrounded by clusters of hard and soft corals, a very typical view of Puerto Galera's coral reefs.*

Above right: *Big La Laguna Beach is one of the most attractive and popular of Puerto Galera's beaches.*

studies centre here as far back as 1934. Almost half a century later, in 1973, the United Nations Education, Science and Cultural Organization (UNESCO) named Puerto Galera's reefs a Man and the Biosphere Marine Reserve. At the same time, the area's forested mountainous hinterland, principally Mounts Malasimbo and Talipanan, were also named a Man and the Biosphere Reserve, thus highlighting the whole Puerto Galera area as a valuable marine and terrestrial environment of global importance.

Whilst the protection given to the terrestrial areas has been less successful, the marine reserve has been well looked after, ensuring that today most of Puerto Galera's reefs are in excellent condition, providing a rich diversity of marine life and, as a result, some of the best diving and snorkelling in the country. Although the university's marine studies centre closed down some time ago research still continues, scientists travelling down from Manila for occasional surveys. The reefs remain protected not through any government protected-area programme but owing to the efforts of local people, fishermen, hotel owners and dive operators cooperating to try to ensure that all parts of the local economy benefit from the undersea riches.

A Popular Resort

The area as a whole focuses on the small town of Puerto Galera, situated at the innermost point of Muelle Bay, a beautiful natural harbour almost completely enclosed by

Location: In Oriental Mindoro province, at the northern tip of Mindoro, about 130 km (80 miles) south of Manila.

Climate: No distinct dry season; rain likely any time of year. But April–May usually driest period. Temperatures usually over 30°C (86°F), although sea breezes make night times quite cool, especially in January. Humidity is always high, usually about 80%.

When to go: Diving on reefs at any time of year; March–October said to be best period.

Access: Bus from Manila to Batangas (three hours), and then a ferry to Puerto Galera (1–2 hours depending on type of ferry). Take a boat, tricycle or jeepney from the Puerto Galera wharf to the beach of choice.

Equipment: Swimwear, sunblock, sunglasses, camera. Diving and snorkelling equipment can be hired, but divers can bring their own if they prefer.

Facilities: Accommodation at the beaches. Most dive operators are based at Sabang and Big and Small La Laguna Beaches, also a few at White Beach. Most run a range of diving courses from novice to instructor level. Hire boats for diving, snorkelling, swimming or touring.

Wildlife: Vast array of corals and diversity of fish including: Butterflyfish, Moorish Idols, sweetlips, soldierfish all common. Huge barrel sponges found at some dive sites.

Visitor Activities: Exploring the beaches by boat or foot; swimming; snorkelling; diving.

Above: *A dive boat moored close to the shore at Big La Laguna Beach.*

Right: *A Linckia starfish, a very common inhabitant of Puerto Galera's reefs.*

a peninsula to the east and a cluster of islands, Boquete and San Antonio, to the west. Arriving here by ferry from Luzon is a memorable experience, as the ship sails past a series of headlands into the hidden Muelle Bay, a sparkling aquamarine expanse of water surrounded by low hills stunningly green in their cloak of coconut palms. Brilliant white yachts lie at anchor scattered across the innermost parts of the bay, while in the background looms Mount Malasimbo, a brooding deep green, invariably covered in a heavy blanket of cloud.

On arrival at the wharf one is hardly aware of the town – just a few roofs visible through coconut palms and a line of small shops and cafes along the waterfront giving its presence away. In any case, few visitors stay in the town long, almost all being whisked away by boat or vehicle to any one of the beaches that lie to the east and west. Those intent on exploring the coral reefs usually head eastwards to the beaches of Big and Small La Laguna or Sabang, lying at the outermost end

of the Puerto Galera peninsula, though there are also beaches to the west, such as White Beach, where there is some diving available.

Diving on the Coral Reefs

Most of the coral reefs lie off the northern coastline of the peninsula, within easy reach of some of the main beaches. The submarine terrain varies from gently sloping and shallow coral gardens with a sandy floor, to steep rocky drop-offs or vertical walls descending into deep water. Moreover, with the coastline consisting of so many islands, inlets and headlands, the degree of exposure varies enormously from place to place, leaving some reefs in calm, sheltered waters, and others exposed to the open sea and strong tidal currents.

The result of such varied terrain and exposure is a great diversity of marine life, ranging from large expanses of hard corals in the shallow areas, such as Acropora table and staghorn corals, populated with shoals of tiny reef fish such as soldierfish, sergeant majors and butterflyfish, to large Gorgonian sea-fans, *Tubastraea* cup corals and barrel sponges in the deeper,

more exposed places where currents often run fast and fierce. Here shoals of larger reef fish are found, such as triggerfish, parrotfish, wrasse and sweetlips, as well as deep water pelagics, including barracuda, tuna and occasionally sharks, mostly Whitetip Reef Sharks. Moray Eels lurk in the crevasses found on many of the rocky slopes and walls, while rays are common in the sandy areas. Everywhere, soft corals are abundant, including delicately branching and often vividly coloured soft tree corals, large and lobed mushroom leather corals and the delicately 'leaved' palm corals.

A string of dive sites has become well established, covering all these habitats and conditions, those close inshore and in shallow, sheltered waters benefiting the novice diver and snorkeller, those further out in the exposed waters of Verde Island Passage appealing to divers with more experience. Many of the dive sites' names reflect local conditions or the dive's main high-light, from such mild places as Coral Garden or Sweetlips Cave to the rougher sites that include The Canyons, Shark Cave or The Washing Machine, the last of these so named for the violence of its currents!

Above: *A trio of Moorish Idols swim past clusters of coral.*

Below: *The hard, brittle spikes of an* Acropora *hard coral, widespread across the reefs in shallower water.*

SIBUYAN ISLAND & MOUNT GUITING GUITING NATURAL PARK

An Island Wilderness

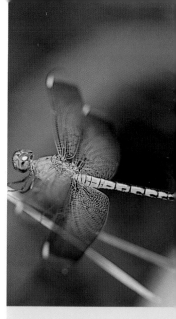

Situated in the north of the Visayas, the rather isolated island of Sibuyan has one of the most intact natural environments in the entire country. This ranges from coral reefs offshore through beach and mangrove forests along the shoreline, to lowland, montane and mossy forests as one travels inland and climbs ever higher up the slopes of Mount Guiting Guiting, a huge mountain that dominates the island's landscape. Only recently recognized as critical to the conservation of Philippine biodiversity, Sibuyan's mountainous interior was declared a natural park in 1996 and is now part of the European Union-funded National Integrated Protected Areas Programme (NIPAP).

A Magnificent Emerald Isle

Covering an area of 450 square kilometres (180 square miles), the island is dominated by Mount Guiting Guiting, which rises directly from the coastal plain to a height of 2,050 metres (6,725 feet). From its lowest slopes up to Mayo's Peak, a secondary summit at 1,550 metres (5,000 feet), the mountain is covered in primary forest,

Opposite: *The clear waters of the Cantingas River pour away from the southern slopes of Mt Guiting Guiting.*

Above right: *A damselfly found in swamp forest close to Sibuyan's southwest coast.*

although from this point up to the main summit the rugged terrain consists only of grass and bare rock. From Mayo's Peak down to approximately 1,350 metres (4,400 feet) the steep slopes are cloaked in mossy forest, a region of stunted trees draped in ferns, orchids and moss, while below this – down to approximately 650 metres (2,100 feet) – is montane forest, characterized by much taller, straighter trees, draped in vines and climbing bamboo, and interspersed with pandanus plants, rattans and tree ferns. Below 650 metres (2,100 feet) is lowland rainforest, the land of the giant dipterocarp trees.

Originally the lowland forest stretched right across the narrow coastal plain that encircles Mount Guiting Guiting, but extensive logging from the 1940s until 1992 cleared almost all of this, although patches still survive on the mountain's lower slopes. In some parts of the coastal plain the lowland forest has started to regenerate, to the point that secondary forest now reaches all the way to the shore, merging with extensive mangroves. The mangroves in turn give way to seagrass and seaweed beds in the shallow waters, which themselves in deeper water are replaced by a coral reef that encircles much of the island. Along the island's southwest coast, mangroves are replaced by specialized beach forest.

For the 47,000 local residents life is basic, consisting

MAP LABELS:
Sibuyan Sea · Point Casing · Magdiwang · Lambingan Falls · Cataja Falls · Mountt Guiting Guiting Natural Park · Agtiwa · 1550m (5086ft) Mayo's Peak · Mt Guiting Guiting 2050m (6726ft) · Marigondon · Sibuyan Island · España · Cajidiocan · Manila · Cantingas River · Lagting Falls · San Fernando · Romblon Passage · Malaysia · Cauit Point

Location: In the Sibuyan Sea, about 75 km (47 miles) northeast of Panay and 60 km (37 miles) west of Masbate.

Climate: Rain throughout the year, but mostly July–December. Driest and hottest April–May. In lowlands daytime temperatures range from 28°C/82°F (January) to 34°C/93°F (May). In the mountains, temperature quickly drops with altitude, falling to about 10°C (50°F), or lower when wet, at the summit.

When to go: Climb Guiting Guiting in April or May, when rainfall at lowest. Explore the lowlands at any time; reasonable weather January–May.

Access: By bus from Manilla to Batangas then ferry, which leaves at 7 pm daily except Wednesdays. Ferry journey takes 16 hours and stops at two other islands. Arrives in Magdiwang mid-morning.

Equipment: Full camping equipment and food if climbing Mt Guiting Guiting. Good walking shoes, sunblock, insect repellent, leech socks, camera, binoculars.

Facilities: Guides for hire at park headquarters; motorized tricycles in Magdiwang for lowland tours; accommodation limited: couple of homestays in Magdiwang.

Wildlife: Shorebirds seen in the mangroves; raptors seen over the forest. Small farmland and forest birds can be seen in regenerating lowland forest. Wildlife difficult to see in dense forest on mountain.

Visitor Activities: Motorized tours of the lowland areas, birdwatching, hiking.

Above: *Brahminy Kites, frequently seen along Sibuyan's coasts.*

Above right: *Patches of swamp forest adapted to living in marshy condtions, common along Sibuyan's southwest coast.*

Right: *The Rufous Night-heron is rare in the Philippines, but the mangroves of Sibuyan are one place where they can be found.*

Below: *A damselfly found in swamp forest close to Sibuyan's southwest coast.*

of subsistence agriculture and fishing. Almost everyone lives along the coasts, concentrated into three towns, Magdiwang, Cajidiocan and San Fernando. Population growth remains very low, something that has helped preserve the island's natural environment.

Wildlife on the Mountain

The deep waters surrounding Sibuyan have ensured its prolonged isolation, even during the last Ice Age. As a result, it is usually considered a distinct biogeographic zone, as reflected in its mammalian wildlife. Mount Guiting Guiting has been found to harbour no less than five species of mammal unique to the island, four of them small rodents and the fifth a fruit bat. Several other species endemic to the Philippines have been found on Sibuyan, including four fruit bats. One of these, the Philippine Tube-nosed Fruit Bat, was – until recently discovered on Sibuyan – thought to survive only on Negros. Commoner mammals include the Malay Civet and Long-tailed Macaque.

The island's birdlife consists of 131 species, of which 102 are believed to breed here. Birds that can be seen even without climbing to the heights of Guiting Guiting include the Rufous Night-heron, Brahminy Kite, Wandering Whistling-duck, Blue-naped Parrot and Black-naped Oriole.

Along the shores, Green and Hawksbill Turtles still regularly nest on the beaches, while Olive Ridley, Leatherback and Loggerhead Turtles can be seen occasionally. A few Dugong are present in coastal waters.

Conserving the Island

The protection given to Mount Guiting Guiting came about as a result of a local campaign, fuelled by islanders' fears that excessive logging and harvesting of materials within the forest would destroy the resources on which their already meagre livelihoods depended. Since the creation in 1996 of the protected area and integration into NIPAP, plans have been put forward to extend the park's boundaries to cover far more of the island's natural treasures. With the park presently covering only 15,700 hectares (38,800 acres), limited to the slopes of Mount Guiting Guiting, most of the lowland forest and all of the mangroves and beach forest fall only

within one of the buffer zones, and hence are not fully protected. It is hoped that this will soon be put right.

Exploring Sibuyan

For those keen to climb Mount Guiting Guiting, a trail starts from the park headquarters, close to the north coast and just east of Magdiwang. Although it starts off easily enough, passing through regenerating lowland forest on the coastal plain, it becomes an extremely steep climb, and the round trip requires about three to four days. Alternatively, the return climb to Mayo's Peak take only 24 hours and it is possible to camp overnight and enjoy some of the simply stunning views.

In the lowlands it is possible to visit a number of waterfalls and explore some of the lowland forest. A few kilometres east of Magdiwang are the Lambingan Falls, the most accessible of all the waterfalls, while a couple of hours' hike to the southwest of the town is Sibuyan's largest waterfall, Cataja Falls, a huge cascade pouring down in several levels through the forest. In the southeast of the island, near San Fernando, is the attractive Lagting Falls, while a little to the west is Cantingas River, a beautiful ribbon of clear water flowing out of the mountains.

Other explorations can take in the mangroves of the north coast and the beach forests of the southwest, as well as some swamp forest, an area of marshy lowland complete with its own specialized forest. Unfortunately, there is no dive operation on the island.

Above: *Beach forest lines a quiet lagoon on Sibuyan Island's southwest coast.*

Left: *A mudskipper, the ubiquitous resident of mangroves, hauls itself up onto a rock at low tide.*

MOUNT KANLAON NATURAL PARK

The Visayas' Highest Mountain

Situated in the central-northern region of Negros, Mount Kanlaon is one of six volcanoes that form the Negros Volcanic Belt, part of which is submarine but whose bulk is visible as Negros's mountainous spine. Kanlaon is presently the only active volcano in this chain, its last eruption having been in 1996.

Consisting of dense rainforest as well as the volcano, and covering an area of 24,600 hectares (60,700 acres), this is one of the Philippines' ten priority protected areas, a group of the country's most important parks in the Integrated Protected Areas System (IPAS), established in the mid-1990s. However, unlike most of the other priority protected areas, Mount Kanlaon has been a reserve for some time, having been proclaimed a national park as far back as 1934.

A Wild and Primeval Landscape

This highly active volcano is defined as a stratovolcano, which means it has the potential for serious, violent eruptions. In fact, although it has erupted frequently, in recent history all eruptions have thankfully been quite small ones.

Opposite: *The gaping chasm that is the active crater of Mt Kanlaon, the highest mountain and most active volcano in the Visayas.*

Above right: *Signs encouraging respect for nature at Mambucal hot spring resort.*

As with most Philippine volcanoes, the terrain is extremely steep, culminating in the active crater at the summit, variously reported as between 2,438 and 2,465 metres (7,999–8,088 feet) high, making it the highest mountain in the Visayan region. The active crater is a fearsome sight, a gaping hole estimated to be 500 metres (1,640 feet) across, with sheer walls that plunge directly into an apparently bottomless funnel from which curls a small but constant plume of smoke and steam. There is no flat area around the rim of the crater; instead the outer slopes leading up to it end abruptly in a knife-edge rim that actually overhangs the chasm. There is no vegetation here, only grey volcanic rock, the loose gravelly surface making it essential to take care while walking.

North of this crater is an old, inactive crater known as the Margaha Valley. Now green and pleasant, its southern end is carpeted with grass which turns into a lake approximately a metre (3 feet) deep during the rainy season. Further north again is a secondary peak, Mount Makawiwili, and beyond this the mountain slowly descends in a series of steps marked by ancient volcanic craters, now mostly beautiful lakes, towards the hot spring resort of Mambucal.

Conserving the Forest and Its Wildlife

Since 1934, half of the park's 24,600 hectares (60,700 acres) has been converted to farmland by encroaching settlers. However, the remaining 11,500 hectares

---

Map labels:
To Bacolod · Murcia · Manila · Negros · Malaysia · Bago · Hot Springs · Mambucal · Mount Kanlaon Natural Park · San Carlos · Guintubdan · La Carlota · San Enrique · Mt Kanlaon 2465m (8088ft) · Pontevedra · Kanlaon · Vallehermosa · La Castellana · NEGROS · Hinigaran · Tanon Strait · Binalbagan · Magallon · Himamaylan · Guihulngan · N

Location: Central-northern Negros, approximately 30 km (19 miles) southeast of Bacolod.

Climate: Dry season from January–May. Heavy rains from June–December. Temperatures at base of mountain range from 30°C/86°F to 37°C/96°F, falling quickly with altitude to about 15°C/59°F at 1,500 metres (4,900 feet) and lower at the summit.

When to go: Climb only in the dry season. The mountain is closed to hikers during the rains.

Access: Daily flights from Manila to Bacolod. From here take a shuttle bus to La Carlota and then a jeepney to Guintubdan. Return to Bacolod from Mambucal by jeepney.

Permits: From Natural Park office in Bacolod. Permits checked at the park office in Guintubdan.

Equipment: Good walking boots, full camping equipment, food and fuel, waterproof and warm clothing, leech socks, insect repellent, binoculars.

Facilities: Hire guides and porters through the Department of Tourism office in Bacolod. Camping grounds at Guintubdan and five sites along the route. The trails are very basic and unmaintained. Hotels and hot springs (excellent) in Mambucal.

Wildlife: Dipterocarp, montane and mossy forests, with a range of flowering plants, rattans and vines. Animal wildlife difficult to spot, but some forest birds are visible. Fruit bats at Mambucal.

Visitor Activities: Soaking in the hot springs, hiking, photography.

(28,400 acres) are still densely forested, and include the three main bands of forest, namely lowland evergreen forest, montane forest and mossy forest. Although rather fragmented by agricultural encroachment and further damaged on the mountain's northern slopes by the recent construction of a geothermal plant, parts of the lowland forest still consist of the characteristic triple canopy. The tallest trees, as much as 37 metres (120 feet) high and forming the upper canopy, are the dipterocarps, consisting of *Shorea* and *Parashorea* species, in the Philippines commonly known by such names as Lauan, White Lauan and Tanguile, all important timber trees now quite rare owing to the massive and chronic logging that has occurred throughout the country. Below these is a layer of shorter trees, up to 20 metres (65 feet) high, which make up the majority of the forest's tree species. The third and lowest canopy consists of immature trees of both these groups.

At approximately 1,000 metres (3,300 feet) this forest gives way to montane forest, consisting of a two-layer forest of trees up to 20 metres (65 feet) high, as well as large numbers of Pandanus plants, both as free-standing shrubs and climbers, climbing bamboo, rattans and other palms, and a wide variety of vines. Flowering plants can sometimes be seen, especially the now quite rare *Medinilla magnifica*, known locally as Kapa-Kapa, an epiphyte with clusters of pink flowers that usually hang down from the trees above. As one climbs higher and rainfall increases, so does the amount of moss on the trees. Above approximately 1,800 metres (5,900 feet) one is in the realm of the mossy forest, consisting of only a single storey of dwarf trees, draped in mosses. There is also a wealth of other vegetation, including pitcher plants, staghorn and ribbon ferns, and orchids, including the rare Waling-Waling more commonly associated with Mindanao.

About 50 species of bird have been identified on the mountain, including the Flame-templed Tree Babbler, rhe White-winged Cuckoo-shrike and the Visayan Tarictic Hornbill, believed to be restricted on Negros to just a few sites. Only 11 species of mammal are so far known in this area, but these include the Visayan Spotted Deer and the Visayan Warty Pig, both highly endangered, as well as the Malay Civet, the Leopard Cat and five species of fruit bat.

Hiking on the Volcano

There are several routes up this mountain. One of the best, which involves camping out for two nights, starts

from the village of Guintubdan on the western slopes. There are several attractive waterfalls in this area, and the village is renowned as the fighting cock breeding capital of Negros – it is hard to imagine so many cockerels in one place! From here the path strikes out into dense montane forest and climbs steeply all the way to the ridge that surrounds the Margaha Valley, leading to the active crater.

After visiting the summit, backtrack along the ridge and then follow a path past the Makawiwili peak and through dense mossy forest towards Samoc Lagoon, remnant of an ancient crater and a beautiful lake with a pleasant camping area. This is an exhausting section of the path as one is constantly climbing over or under low and fallen trees, but as the dense mossy forest is left behind so the trail becomes rather easier, and as it dips down to approximately 800 metres (2,600 feet), so one enters dipterocarp forest.

Reaching the new geothermal installation signals that the hike is nearing its end; a couple of hours later you pass the Wasay entrance to the park and soon are descending into the very pleasant little hot spring resort of Mambucal – the ideal place for a long soak after the exertions of the trail.

Above: *The Margaha Valley, the remains of an old crater, close to the summit of Mt Kanlaon.*

Left: *A wild hydrangea in flower in Kanlaon's dense montane forest.*

Left: *Wild ginger in flower in dense montane forest.*

Opposite: *Magasawang Falls, a gem hidden in the forest just a few minutes' walk from Guintubdan.*

BALICASAG ISLAND MARINE RESERVE

Submarine Cliffs Teeming with Life

This is a tiny island lying southwest of Bohol, about eight kilometres (five miles) from Panglao Island, site of Alona Beach, Bohol's most popular beach resort. The island itself is flat and low-lying, covered with coconut palms and rough scrub, but it is ringed by a dazzlingly white beach and beyond that by some of the Philippines' most stunning submarine scenery. A narrow coral reef, surrounding much of the island, ends abruptly in massive walls that drop into deep water, teeming with life. These waters became a marine reserve in 1986, and include a fish sanctuary on the southwestern side in which no fishing of any kind is allowed.

A Tiny Desert Island

A rather featureless piece of land, Balicasag is a perfectly flat, almost round island, barely 600 metres (650 yards) in diameter and covering an area of approximately 30 hectares (75 acres). Despite its isolation from

Opposite above: *The shore of Balicasag Island, surrounded by a dazzling white beach.*

Opposite below left: *Detail of a beautiful, translucent* Dendronephthya *soft tree coral.*

Opposite below right: *A deadly scorpionfish lies close against the rock and coral, extremely well camouflaged against its background.*

Above right: *A Fromia* starfish, *common inhabitants of Balicasag's coral reefs.*

Panglao Island, it is inhabited by about 60 families, who inevitably make their living from fishing. Although these people have come to live here at some point in the past 50 years, the island has been occupied since the 1870s, when a watchtower was built to guard Bohol against Moslem attacks from Mindanao. To this day the island remains a naval reserve, administered by the Philippine Coastguard. A small lighthouse was built on the island in 1907, a beacon that still lights the sea lanes for shipping travelling to and from Cebu.

For the visitor, apart from a small resort run by the Philippine Tourist Authority, the only interesting feature of the island itself is the astonishingly white beach made of coralline sand, billions of tiny white fragments of the reef that encircles the island. The beach is particularly fine close to the resort, making an excellent base from which to go snorkelling.

Conservation of the Island's Waters

The fringing reef, walls and drop-offs that surround Balicasag have long been recognized for their vast range of marine life. As early as the 1970s the area was recommended as a possible marine park, but little happened until 1984 when staff from the Marine Laboratory at Silliman University, based in Dumaguete on Negros, began their Marine Conservation and Development Programme. This consisted of community work aimed at encouraging the local populations of three islands –

Location: Approximately 8 km (5 miles) southwest of Duljo Point on Panglao Island, Bohol, at 9°31'N 123°41'E.

Climate: Dry season lasts from January–June, with rains for rest of year. Peak rainy season August–November; driest in April and May. Daytime temperatures range from 30°C (86°F) to 35°C (95°F), hottest month is May.

When to go: For diving, the high season is November to May. Strong northeast winds can sometimes make diving around Balicasag difficult in December–February. The calmest months are April–May.

Access: Daily flights from Manila to Cebu, followed by high-speed ferry to Tagbilaran, capital of Bohol. High-speed ferries also run daily to Tagbilaran from Cagayan de Oro and Camiguin Island, Mindanao, and from Dumaguete on Negros. From Tagbilaran take a tricycle or taxi to Alona Beach, and then go with a dive boat.

Equipment: Swimsuit, sunblock, sunglasses, hat, camera. Diving and snorkelling equipment can be hired on Alona Beach or at the Balicasag Island Dive Resort.

Facilities: One resort on Balicasag Island; plenty of accommodation at Alona Beach, Panglao Island. Numerous dive operations on Alona Beach, one at Balicasag Island Dive Resort.

Watching wildlife: A vast array of marine life to be seen underwater, whether diving or snorkelling.

Visitor activities: Sun-bathing, swimming, snorkelling, diving.

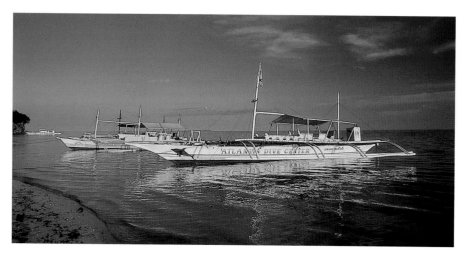

Balicasag, Pamilacan (to the south of Bohol) and Apo (south of Negros) – to launch and maintain their own reserves. The work was successful, resulting in the fishermen of Balicasag establishing their own marine reserve late in 1985, gaining official status in 1986.

The reserve consists of all the waters around the island to a distance of 500 metres (550 yards) offshore, covering an area of 150 hectares (360 acres), along with a fish sanctuary of eight hectares (20 acres) off the southwest shore. Within the former only traditional hand-line and trap methods of fishing are allowed, while in the latter all fishing is banned, providing a sanctuary in which both fish and corals can breed safely, allowing them to spread to adjacent areas of the reef.

The reserve and sanctuary are still policed by the islanders themselves. Visiting dive boats have to pay a fee for the privilege of diving in the reserve and are allowed only to tie up to one of the few buoys placed for the purpose – no anchors are allowed.

Diving Among the Marine Life

The reef begins in the shallows immediately off the island's beach, and extends to a distance of 50–100 metres (55–110 yards) from the shore and to a depth of 7–11 metres (23–36 feet) before the reef crest is reached, followed by a wall or steeply sloping drop-off. Along the southern side of the island the reef terminates at the edge of an absolutely vertical wall, which drops from a depth of about eight metres (26 feet) straight down to 35 metres (115 feet), while on the north side the drop-off is a slope.

The reef is populated with all the usual hard corals, including staghorns, table corals, brain corals, fire corals, fungus and mushroom corals, while on the walls and slopes are multicoloured Gorgonian sea-fans, soft tree corals, whip corals, nudibranchs and sponges. The northern slope is also well known for its forests of black corals, characterized by masses of long coralline 'fronds' or 'tentacles'. In this area the sandy bottom is home to hundreds of garden eels, which partially extend from their homes in the sand, forming a forest of 'sticks' waving in the currents, instantaneously retracting en masse into the sand the moment they are disturbed.

Fish life is truly massive and includes everything from the tiniest gobies to sharks. It is always possible to see a vast range of reef fish, including striped lionfish, multicoloured wrasse, Moorish Idols, small and larger groupers, sweetlips and pufferfish. Frogfish and even scorpionfish, both almost invisible as they crouch low

and almost perfectly colour-matched against their background, are quite common. Banded sea snakes are also a regular sight; although they have never been known to attack divers, they are best left alone.

The deep waters off the reef ensure that large numbers of pelagic fish frequent Balicasag. Shoals of Trevally, jack and barracuda are commonly seen, often forming huge 'walls' of fish, as well as incredible spiral columns, vertical tubes created by hundreds of fish swimming in circles. It is possible for divers to enter these tubes to experience a huge column of fish endlessly circling all around.

Opposite, top: *Dive boats moored at Alona Beach, ready for the next day's dive trips to Balicasag.*

Opposite, bottom: *A novice diver receives training in Balicasag's shallows.*

Above: *Most people intending to visit Balicasag Island stay on Alona Beach, a 45-minute boat ride away.*

Below left: *A diver has an encounter with a Banded Sea-snake off Balicasag Island.*

Below right: *Stinging hydroids are to be avoided as even a gentle brush can give bare skin a very nasty sting.*

Above: *A* Xenia *soft coral, typified by this much-branched form crowned with long, waving polyps and coloured creamy-white is ubiquitous, found on just about every Philippine reef.*

Right: *A shoal of Big-eye Trevally, seen against a high sun, sweep across above the diver, a common sight in the deep waters around Balicasag Island.*

Below: *Living close to the reef, and using its many nooks and crannies for shelter, is a myriad of small, multi-coloured fish.*

SIARGAO ISLAND PROTECTED LANDSCAPES & SEASCAPES

A Varied Archipelago

Lying off the northeastern tip of Mindanao, this protected area consists not just of the island of Siargao itself but also of a cluster of smaller islands and islets as well as much of the surrounding sea. Incorporating beaches, caves, mangroves, lowland rainforest and coral reefs, Siargao Island is recognized to be of major importance to Philippine conservation. As a result, it is one of the 10 priority protected areas that form part of the new Integrated Protected Areas System funded by the World Bank. Although parts of Siargao were protected as early as 1981, the entire area did not become a single protected area until 1996 when it was declared a Protected Landscapes and Seascapes site (a category covering regions in which the human population seems to be living in harmony with the environment and using its resources sustainably), covering an area of 157,375 hectares (388,880 acres).

The Islands of the Protected Area

At 67,725 hectares (167,350 acres), land makes up less than half of the park's total area, the remaining 89,650 hectares (221,530 acres) covering the reefs and fishing grounds of the surrounding seas. The largest landmass by far is Siargao Island itself, while to the south lie Bucas Grande, Bagum and Bancuyo Islands. There is also a host of small islands and islets, such as Daco, Anahawan and Mangantuc, almost all inhabited by at least one community of fishermen. Perhaps the smallest island of all is tiny Guyam, little more than a sand-bar bearing a few coconut palms, set in shallow seas and surrounded by seagrass beds and coral reefs, off the southeastern tip of Siargao.

The east and west coasts of Siargao are quite different. The former is exposed to the full force of the Pacific Ocean, and is characterized by a coastline that alternates between sandy beaches and rocky shorelines, with fringing coral reefs in some of the less exposed areas.

Map labels: Manila; Mindanao; Malaysia; Dinagat Sound; Sugbuhan Point; Santa Monica; Burgos; Dahican Island; San Benito; Halian Island; Mangancub Island; San Isidro; Casulian Island; Poneas Island; Siargao Island; Laonan Island; Del Carmen; Park Office; Pilar; Tona Island; Siargao Island Protected Landscapes and Seascapes; Cloud Nine; General Luna; Bucas Point; Dapa; Lahayay Island; Daco Island; San Miguel; Bagum Island; Bancuyo Island; Casulian Island; Bucas Grande Island; La Januza Island; Pamusaingan; Anahawan Island; Mam-on Island; Socorro; Suhoton Cave; Mangantoa Island; Hinituan Passage

Opposite above: A quiet, sandy cove near Cloud Nine provides a convenient anchorage for local fishing boats, sheltered from the Pacific surf crashing on the distant reef.

Opposite below: Carefully punting a boat through waters too shallow to use the engine, towards tiny Guyam Islet.

Above right: A young fishing family sifts through its net for fish after a sweep through beachside shallows.

Location: Off the northeastern tip of Mindanao, about 50 km (31 miles) from Surigao, the nearest mainland port.

Climate: No completely dry season, but driest month is June. The heaviest rains November–January. Daytime temperatures range from 30°C (86°F) to 35°C (95°F), the hottest time being June. Humidity ranges from 80% to 90%. These islands rarely, if ever, get hit by typhoons.

When to go: April–September offers reasonable weather. July to October is the best time for surfers, as typhoons passing to the north whip up surf here.

Access: Daily flights from Manila to Cebu, followed by high-speed ferry to Surigao in mainland Mindanao. From Surigao daily high-speed ferries run to Dapa, the largest town on Siargao. From other parts of Mindanao, express buses run frequently to Surigao, via Butuan.

Equipment: Walking shoes, swimsuits, sunblock, hat, camera, binoculars, and all diving and surfing equipment.

Facilities: Almost all accommodation is in General Luna and Cloud Nine. Boats can be hired at the Cloud Nine resorts or in General Luna, Del Carmen, Dapa and Socorro (Bucas Grande Island). Snorkelling equipment can be hired.

Wildlife: Coral reefs in shallow water, birds in the mangroves, monitor lizards in the forests and coconut groves.

Visitor Activities: Boat riding, walking, snorkelling, surfing.

Beyond the outer islets, the sea shelves steeply towards the massive Philippine Trench, which reaches a depth of over 10,000 metres (38,000 feet) 80 km (50 miles) northeast of Siargao. The west coast is sheltered by Mindanao to the west, and so is shallow and calm. Here extensive mangroves, especially around the township of Del Carmen, cover an area of 8,600 hectares (21,400 acres), the largest mangrove swamp in Mindanao.

Inland, the landscape is a mixture of plains and low rolling hills, made up of coralline limestone, volcanic rock and alluvial soils. The highest point is just 283 metres (929 feet) above sea level. Agriculture and scrubland cover much of the inland area, plus a number of remnant lowland rainforests. The most extensive surviving forests are to be found on Bucas Grande Island, where there is also the Suhoton Cave, site of an underground river that is slowly becoming popular with visitors.

The population of the protected area is about 82,000, mostly concentrated into the townships of Dapa (the largest settlement), Del Carmen, General Luna, Pilar, San Isidro, Burgos and Santa Monica on Siargao itself. Livelihoods consist almost entirely of subsistence fishing and farming.

Fauna and Flora

Surviving old growth forests cover an area of 4,440 hectares (10,970 acres), while secondary forest takes up another 12,600 hectares (31,135 acres). Both contain dipterocarp trees, while the forests of Bucas Grande Island are also rich in the Ironwood tree, highly prized for its timber and which as a result is now very rare in the rest of the Philippines.

Siargao's fauna includes the Saltwater Crocodile, which lives in the vast mangrove swamp to the west of

Del Carmen. The Dugong and several species of marine turtle visit the more exposed eastern coasts, the latter nesting on some of the isolated beaches, the former feeding on the seagrass beds. On land, the list of animals includes the Philippine Tarsier, Malay Civet, monitor lizards, and at least 84 species of bird, including the endangered Philippine Cockatoo.

Exploring the Islands

Overseas visitors have been making their way to Siargao since the early 1990s, but not for the scenery or the sake of nature conservation. This is a newly discovered surf heaven: the Pacific swell that rolls into the islands' eastern shores sends up enormous waves that create some of the most spectacular surfing conditions anywhere in Southeast Asia. Surf breaks have been discovered up and down the whole of Siargao's east coast, but the most famous is on its southeastern tip, close to the town of General Luna and nicknamed Cloud Nine. Such is the magnetism of this name that it seems to have completely replaced this headland's original title, even among the locals, and any foreign visitor seen anywhere near Siargao is simply assumed to be heading for Cloud Nine.

For those more with scenery in mind, there is plenty of exploring to be done, much of it by boat. Some of the best beaches are around the smaller islands, such as Guyam (where there is also good snorkelling) and Daco, although there are also good beaches at General Luna in the southeast and at Burgos in the north. Pilar, on Siargao's east coast, has the magnificent Magpopongko Rock Formation. On Bucas Grande Island Suhoton Cave can be partially explored, while close by are the Magkahuyog Falls. It is also possible to hire a boat at Del Carmen for an exploration of the mangroves, while almost anywhere on Siargao Island it is possible to hire a motorbike to have a guided tour of the inland areas.

Unfortunately there is no dive operation on Siargao Island, although snorkelling equipment can be hired. Good snorkelling areas can be found by taking boat trips to the areas around Guyam and Daco Islands.

Above: *A mix of hard and soft corals form a healthy reef in the shallow waters off Guyam Islet.*

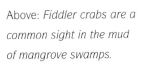

Above: *Fiddler crabs are a common sight in the mud of mangrove swamps.*

MOUNT APO NATURAL PARK

The Philippines' Highest Mountain

At 2,954 metres (9,692 feet), Mount Apo is the Philippines' highest mountain, declared a national park in 1936. The mountain, an inactive volcano, lies west of Davao, in central-southern Mindanao, and covers an area of 72,110 hectares (178,190 acres), encompassing dense rainforests that spread across not just Mount Apo but also neighbouring Mount Talomo. The park is an invaluable refuge for wildlife, including the Philippine Eagle, and is one of the country's 10 priority protected areas. Several trails lead to the summit, and the climb is rapidly becoming one of the country's most popular hiking experiences.

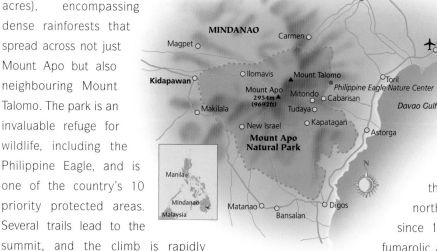

northwestern slopes. This small lake, surrounded by dense forest, is close to boiling point and continually pours off thick clouds of billowing steam. Nearby is a large new geothermal plant that harnesses this energy. It is, controversially, carved out of the forest.

At about 2,400 metres (7,900 feet), nestled on a plateau, is Lake Venado – the remains of Apo's ancient crater, with the summit of Mount Apo lying to the southeast and that of Mount Talomo to the northeast. Apo has not erupted since 1640, but there is still some fumarolic activity just below its summit, with jets of steam and sulphurous smoke emitted from rocks on the steep eastern slopes.

A Mountain Landscape

The mountain rises up from the western shores of Davao Gulf, and while it has relatively gentle slopes on the northern and southern sides, it is very steep to the east and west. As a reminder that this volcano is not dead, there are a number of hot springs, the most accessible of which is Lake Agco, lying at an altitude of approximately 1,200 metres (3,900 feet) on the

Opposite: *A gigantic Almaciga tree, the largest of the Philippines' forest trees, stands on the middle slopes of Mt Apo, shrouded in fog.*

Above right: *The Golden-crowned Flying Fox, one of the world's largest fruit bats, lives in Mt Apo's forests.*

The Mountain's Wildlife

Apo's uppermost 500 metres (1,600 feet) consist of rough and rocky grassland, but from Lake Venado downwards the mountain is covered with rainforest. Down to about 1,500 metres (4,900 feet) this consists of mossy forest, dense stands of gnarled trees with a canopy only 5-10 metres (16–33 feet) high, everything draped in thick layers of moss, ferns, orchids and other epiphytes. From 1,500 metres down to 1,000 metres (3,300 feet) is montane forest, consisting of taller trees, with a canopy about 20 metres (66 feet) high, with some much taller emergent trees. Below 1,000 metres grows lowland rainforest, consisting largely of dipterocarp trees, the giants of the tropical rainforest. Sadly, much of

Location: Immediately west of Davao, straddling North Cotabato province to the west and Davao City to the east.

Climate: Even rainfalls over the year, although April–May drier. Daytime temperatures in Davao 30–35°C (86–95°F). At Lake Agco 15–20°C (59–68°F), and around Lake Venado and the summit 10°C (50°F); lower when raining.

When to go: Climb mountain at any time of year but April–May is driest and sunniest.

Access: Daily flights from Manila and Cebu to Davao. Express buses from northern Mindanao to Davao. Express bus from Davao to Kidapawan (2 hours), followed by jeepney to Lake Agco.

Permits: From the Kidapawan Tourism Council for climbing from Lake Agco.

Equipment: All camping equipment; hiking boots, food, warm and rainproof clothing and rucksack, leech socks, binoculars.

Facilities: Accommodation in Davao and Kidapawan. Small lodge and campsite at Lake Agco. Philippine Eagle Nature Center at Malagos, near Davao. Guides and porters available at Lake Agco.

Wildlife: Parrots around Lake Venado. Philippine Eagles, other raptors, hornbills and some mammals at the Philippine Eagle Nature Center. Wild birds, including Silvery Kingfishers, can be seen in the garden.

Visitor Activities: Philippine Eagle Nature Center, exploring Lake Agco, birdwatching, hiking.

Right: *Philippine Eagles, although highly endangered, are scattered throughout the forests of Mindanao, including those on Mount Apo.*

the lowland forest has been badly damaged owing to an ever-growing number of immigrant farmers.

The higher levels of forest remain in pristine condition, however, and in the montane zone there are stands of Almaciga, a Philippine endemic which, under the right conditons, grows to heights of 60 metres (200 feet), making it the country's biggest tree. Highly prized for both its timber and its resin, across the Philippines this tree has been heavily exploited and is now becoming rare. Here, on Mount Apo, although some have been lost, there are still extensive healthy stands.

Among the animal wildlife, 227 vertebrate species have been identified. Mammals include Philippine Deer, Philippine Warty Pig, Long-tailed Macaque, Philippine Flying Lemur and two species of civet cat. Small mammals include the Mindanao Tree Shrew, Mindanao Flying Squirrel and fruit bats such as the Golden-crowned Flying Fox; the world's largest.

Of the birds found on Mount Apo, 61 species are endemic to the Philippines, 14 of them restricted to Mindanao. The most famous of all is the Philippine Eagle, which is known to nest in and around the park. Over one metre (3 feet) tall and with a wingspan of about two metres (6 feet), this is the second largest raptor in the world, beaten only on weight by the

Harpy Eagle of South America. A forest bird, its rapidly shrinking habitat has left the eagle endangered, with populations surviving only in remote areas of Mindanao, Samar and northern Luzon. Despite several studies, little is known about the bird, and estimates of the number surviving vary from as few as 200 to as many as 2,000.

Conservation Work

The Mount Apo area is well known for work by the Philippine Eagle Foundation, Inc. (PEFI) in attempting to ensure a safe future for this magnificent bird. Community work aimed at helping people living close to the forest to develop non-destructive livelihoods, coupled with efforts to recruit villagers living near known eagle nesting sites to protect the birds, have had some successes. A captive-breeding programme at Malagos near Mount Apo's eastern foot has been less successful, producing small numbers of chicks. Nevertheless the Philippine Eagle Nature Center has a valuable role in enabling both visitors and locals to get to know this bird at close range.

Climbing Mount Apo

Although there are several routes up the mountain, the most popular is from the west, starting at Lake Agco. To make this climb, first obtain a permit from the tourism office in the town of Kidapawan. Then take a jeepney to

Right: *The Mindanao Writhed Hornbill has only recently been classified as a distinct species, endemic to Mindanao.*

Lake Agco, where there is a campsite and a small lodge, set in forest and close to the hot spring lake. Spend the first night here while guides and porters are organized.

From here, the first step is to pass through the gate to the geothermal plant, and then immediately leave the road and strike out up a track. This soon reaches a ridge, after which the path drops steeply down through forest to the Marbel River. You then follow the river upstream, frequently fording it as the valley becomes narrower and steeper, until a small plateau with a hot spring is reached. This is the last you will see of the river, for at this point the path starts the real climb, a very steep haul straight up the mountain through dense forests all the way to Lake Venado. The night's campsite is on the shore of the lake, with good views of the mountain summit.

Next morning, resume the hike before dawn in order to cover the two-hour climb either before sunrise or at least before the sun climbs high and clouds begin to gather over the mountain. Once at the summit, the view is stupendous, northwards across Lake Venado and the mossy forest towards Mount Talomo, and west down onto the geothermal plant and Lake Agco. This is as high as you can climb in the Philippines.

Above: *The summit of Mount Apo seen on a clear morning. It is important to reach the summit early in the morning, as on most days cloud and rain will arrive before lunchtime.*

Below: *Climbing Mount Apo involves numerous fordings of the Marbel River, not always an easy task.*

Top: *Lake Agco, surrounded by Mount Apo's forest, is a natural hot spring lake with a temperature close to boiling.*

Above: *After climbing Mount Apo, there is nothing quite as soothing as a soak in the hot spring bath adjacent to Lake Agco.*

Right: *The view from the summit of Mount Apo, across forest, Lake Venado and Mount Talomo.*

St Paul's Underground River National Park

A Unique Flooded Cave Surrounded by Forest

Situated on Palawan's west coast 81 kilometres (50 miles) north of Puerto Princesa, the provincial capital, this well-protected national park, also known as St Paul's Subterranean National Park, is site of some interesting limestone rainforest, stunning coastal scenery and an underground river. The river runs for eight kilometres (five miles) through a limestone cave before flowing into a lagoon separated from the sea by a beach. It is surrounded by densely forested rugged limestone scenery, through which pass a number of trails that are worth exploring. Established in 1971 and today managed by the Palawan Council for Sustainable Development (PCSD), the park covers an area of 5,750

hectares (14,210 acres), along with a 290 hectare (720 acre) marine sector that protects the shoreline and offshore coral reefs.

A Rugged Limestone Terrain

The area is surrounded by steep limestone hills and dominated by the 1,028 metre (3,373 feet) Mount St Paul's, which lies within the park's boundaries. The mountain obtained its name from British sailors aboard the HMS Royalist, which explored this coast in 1850. Apparently the mountain's dome-shaped outline reminded them of London's St Paul's Cathedral.

Today the park is high on the list of Palawan visitor attractions, although the place is much more than just a tourist site. Its dense forest is of immense importance to the area's wildlife, even though much of the land beyond the park's boundaries is also still forested. At the human level it is also the ancestral domain of one of the Philippines' smallest cultural minorities, the Batak tribe. Now numbering at most only 350 people, this group is in imminent danger of assimilation by the growing number of settlers in the area.

The source of the underground river is the Cabayugan River, one of several watercourses that drain the hills of the interior. The water filters through the porous limestone into caves within the mountains before

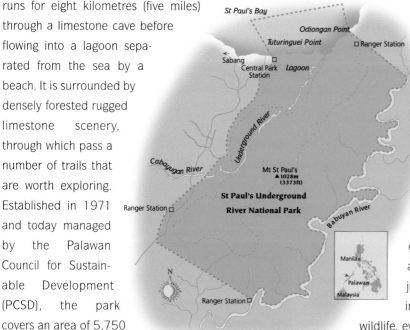

Opposite above: *The coastline of St Paul's Underground River National Park is a mixture of rocky foreshore and white beach, backed by dense forest.*

Opposite below: *The entrance to the Underground River is little more than a relatively small hole in a limestone cliff.*

Above right: *For those hiking into the park, a welcoming sign stands at the point where the path leaves the beach and enters dense rainforest.*

Location: On the west coast of Palawan, 81 km (50 miles) north of Puerto Princesa and 4 km (2.5 miles) east of the coastal village of Sabang.

Climate: Rainy season late May or early June to September or October. Dry season from November–May. Daytime temperatures range from 30–35°C (86–95°F). Coolest in January, hottest in May.

When to go: Dry season. Road to Sabang from Puerto Princesa impassable in heavy rain. Best time February–April.

Access: Daily flights from Manila to Puerto Princesa. From here, some hotels and tour operators offer daily tours to Sabang and the park. A travel agency, Go Palawan, runs a daily minibus to Sabang. Public transport consists of slow and unreliable jeepneys. From Sabang walk into the park or hire a boat at Sabang wharf.

Permits: Obtain at the national park office in Puerto Princesa or at the ranger station in Sabang.

Equipment: Walking shoes, torch (flashlight), insect repellent, anti-malaria prophylactics, swimsuit.

Facilities: Accommodation in Puerto Princesa and Sabang; easily hired boats from Sabang to the park; well-laid trails in the forest; organized exploration of the underground river by boat.

Wildlife: Macaques, monitor lizards, insectivorous bats, Tabon Scrubfowl, swiftlets, forest birds.

Visitor activities: Birdwatching, swimming, cave exploration by boat, hiking.

forming a river that flows towards the sea through the -kilometre (5-mile) cave. The river finally sees the light of day, exiting through the cave's mouth, a 6-metre (20-foot) high opening in a vertical and very jagged limestone cliff. The water flows into a lagoon separated from the sea by a sand-bar, but through which the water is able to flow to reach the sea.

Teeming with Wildlife

The lagoon is surrounded by dense rainforest, which stretches all the way from the beach right up into the furthest mountains, most of it adapted to life on the thin, dry soils that typically cover limestone areas. This is lowland evergreen rainforest, containing many dipterocarp

trees, although here, owing to the thin soil, few reach the gigantic sizes normally associated with these trees. Animal life abounds, the most obvious being the large numbers of Long-tailed Macaques that live in the forest near the lagoon and beach. Two-metre (6-feet) long monitor lizards are also a common sight, often seen swimming across the lagoon. Other mammals include the Asian Short-clawed Otter, although it is most unusual for these shy animals to be seen. The park's caves are home to an uncountable number of insectivorous bats, which stream out in huge crowds at dusk in search of food. They share them with swiftlets, which fly during the daytime, returning to the caves at dusk, at about the same time that the bats leave.

Other birdlife, concentrated in the forest, include Hill Mynahs, a bird valued in the pet trade for its ability to talk and which as a result is now locally endangered; the Tabon Scrubfowl, a chicken-like bird that scratches around in the leaf-litter and surface soil for food, and which is remarkable for the huge mound of soil that it builds over its incubating eggs; and the Asian Fairy Bluebird, a gorgeous iridescent blue-and-black bird that is spread across much of Southeast Asia. The Palawan Peacock-pheasant, unique to this island, is also present in the forests of St Paul's, but being a shy, nervous bird the chances of finding one are very remote.

Cave and Forest Exploration

The park is reached from Puerto Princesa via the village of Sabang, located just a few kilometres west of the park and itself site of a spectacular and largely deserted beach. From here one can enter the park either on foot or by boat. The former takes one along the beach and

then, once inside the park, through dense forest on a well-made path all the way to the lagoon, a distance of about 4 kilometres (2½ miles). Alternatively, boats can be hired at Sabang's wharf, for a 15-minute journey into St Paul's Bay, where the boat drops you at a beach. From here, it is a short 200-metre (220-yard) walk through forest to the lagoon.

On the shore of the lagoon rangers check permits and then arrange for outrigger boats to carry visitors into the cave, travelling 1 kilometre (½ mile) along the tunnel before turning around and returning. Each boat carries a powerful lamp, making it possible to see some of the stalactite and stalagmite formations, as well as the huge size of the cave through which the boats travel.

Outside, several well-marked trails allow for exploration of the forest without the need for a guide, two of the most popular routes being the Jungle and Monkey Trails. Macaques, monitor lizards and a range of forest birds are commonly seen. Tabon Scrubfowl are very common around the picnic area, just within the forest on the edge of the beach. Their huge nests can often be seen nearby.

Above: *Boats moored offshore at Sabang beachwith Mt St Paul's behind.*

Below left: *A group of visitors explores the Underground River in a canoe.*

Below: *The Palawan Peacock Pheasant is a spectacular bird, and hard to find in the forest.*

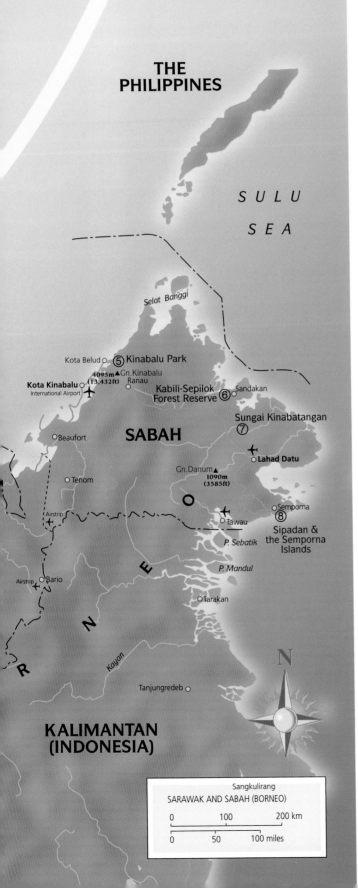

THE
PHILIPPINES

SULU

SEA

Selat Banggi

Kota Belud ○ ⑤ Kinabalu Park

4095m ▲ Gn.Kinabalu
Kota Kinabalu ○ (13,432ft) Ranau
International Airport ✈   Kabili-Sepilok   ○ Sandakan
                      Forest Reserve ⑥ ○

                                Sungai Kinabatangan
                                      ⑦
○ Beaufort   SABAH

                         ✈ ○ Lahad Datu
          Gn.Danum ▲
○ Tenom   1090m
                 (3585ft)
                             ○ Semporna
✈ Airstrip   ⑧
              ✈ ○ Tawau   Sipadan &
          P. Sebatik   the Semporna
                              Islands

                   P. Mandul

Airstrip ○ Bario
    ✈

                   ○ Tarakan

○ Tanjungredeb

**KALIMANTAN
(INDONESIA)**

N

Sangkulirang
SARAWAK AND SABAH (BORNEO)

0   100   200 km

0   50   100 miles

MALAYSIA

Peninsular Malaysia has a coastline of 2,016 kilometres (1,252 miles), including all the smaller offshore islands. Of the Peninsula's parks the biggest is Taman Negara, renowned the world over for its rain forests and exceptionally rich wildlife. It also contains the Peninsula's highest mountain, Gunung Tahan. The Peninsula's parks include seas and islands –the Pulau Redang group just one important area whose spectacular coral reefs and marine life are now protected.

Sarawak is the biggest of Malaysia's 13 states, occupying the northern quarter of the island of Borneo. It has large areas of peat swamp forest on the coastal plains, strange heath forest on areas of poor soils, oxbow lakes, and fantastically high plant diversity. Each of its parks has some special feature; Bako and Gunung Mulu have spectacular rock formations, one of sandstone, the other of limestone, offering incomparable contrasts.

Sabah is the second biggest state of Malaysia and occupies the northeastern corner of Borneo. The coastline is highly indented and convoluted, with many capes, bays and mangrove areas and includes marine parks such as Sipadan, which has some of the best coral reefs in the world. In the east, Sungai Kinabatangan, one of the longest rivers in Malaysia, has oxbow lakes, a broad floodplain, seasonally flooded forest, freshwater dolphins, and important riverine habitats that support large animals. In the predominantly hilly north and west is Gunung Kinabalu, the highest mountain in Malaysia. Here, the visitor can see Proboscis Monkeys, Orang-utans, Rafflesia flowers, and the weirdly shaped pitcher plants.

Above: Geometrid moths include some day-flying forms that have spectacular colouring.

ENDAU ROMPIN NATIONAL PARK

Between the Rivers and the Hills

Amongst the most isolated of Malaysia's mountain groups is that contained in one of its newest parks, Endau Rompin, established in 1989. The park covers 800 square kilometres (300 square miles), of which 489 square kilometres (189 square miles) are in Johor and the rest (known as Rompin Endau) is in Pahang. One reason why the Endau Rompin area is important is the presence of the Sumatran Rhinoceros. A few are still left here, but a sighting is very unlikely for any visitor. However, other big mammals, including elephants, tigers, leopards and Sambar Deer, occur and more than 200 species of birds have been recorded.

Notable features of Endau Rompin are the great variety of forest types supported by the granite-derived valleys, the sandstone hilltop plateaux, the cliffs and swampy patches. Also important are the plants, some unique to the park. About a dozen plants have been described from here within the last 15 years, by far the

Opposite, top: The waters of the Sungai Endau can be of exceptional clarity.

Opposite, bottom left: Tigers, in small numbers, range throughout the park, in the forest and along trails.

Opposite, bottom centre: The lizard Calotes emma is gradually extending its range southwards.

Opposite, bottom right: River trips form an exciting part of the Endau Rompin experience.

Above, right: Endau Rompin is popular with the adventure-minded; many treks are physically demanding.

biggest and most spectacular of which is the fan-palm, *Livistona endauensis*. Others include several small herbs of the African violet family, and a beautiful little understorey tree with coppery coloured foliage.

The Johor Sector

Most visitors to the park arrive by four-wheel drive over dirt roads that were once logging tracks, giving access to the village of Kampung Peta. The people here are known as Orang Hulu, and their language is significantly different from the Malay spoken by their neighbours. From the village and park headquarters the best way into the park is by boat. Along the way it is often possible to see Long-tailed Macaques or a monitor lizard near the riverbank. Look for the cliffs, just visible as a line through the forest as though drawn with a ruler, along the flank of Gunung Janing.

At Kuala Jasin, the Sungai Endau and Sungai Jasin meet in a rocky and rather dangerous confluence, but just upstream there are some delightful bathing spots. From here, various trails can take the visitor, depending on stamina, to the riverine forest of Kuala Marong, the rapids of Jeram Upeh Guling, the waterfall of Buaya Sangkut, the hilltop of Gunung Janing, or – for the very determined – the distant plateau known as Padang Temambung.

At Kuala Marong, an hour's walk from the park headquarters, a scrap of alluvial forest supports some characteristic species, such as the Grey-breasted Babbler. One of the most striking features at Kuala Marong is the extraordinary clarity of the river there. It is shallow enough to paddle over comfortably. Nearby is the little mid-river island of Pulau Jasin, one of the botanical curiosities of the

Location: In the southeast of Peninsular Malaysia, on the border of the states of Johor and Pahang, surrounded by the square of towns Segamat, Keluang, Mersing and Rompin.

Climate: Hot by day, usually warm by night, scattered days of rain throughout the year but, in general, more November–March.

When to Go: Any time of year, but occasional flooding of rivers more likely February–March.

Access: By road from Kuala Lumpur or Singapore to Keluang, then east to beyond Kahang Baharu, and north to Kampung Nitar. Less easily by road from Kahang to Kampung Peta (4-wheel drive needed). From Kampung Nitar or Kampung Peta, about 1 hour by boat to accommodation.

Permits: Must be arranged with National Parks Corporation (Johor) in Johor Bahru. If you are travelling with a tour operator, they may do this on your behalf.

Equipment: Light clothing, walking shoes, swimwear, poncho. Food and basic camping equipment.

Facilities: No luxuries, but Endau Rompin good for camping. River activities and longer treks. Trails lead to main places of interest. Guides from Kampung Peta.

Wildlife: Birdwatching; along trails, look out for elephants, tigers and other big mammals.

Visitor Activities: Camping, swimming (bearing in mind fast currents), birdwatching, walking, fording rivers, photography.

Above: *Along the park's rivers, the vegetation can be rich in orchids and pitcher plants.*

park. Periodically ripped over by floodwaters, the island still supports tough little trees and other plants, including various montane species which have managed to find a foothold just a few hundred metres above sea level. Abundant pitcher plants and orchids add to the montane atmosphere. On the trees are many epiphytes, some such as the Monkey's Head providing an internal network of passages which ants use for their nests.

Just upstream from the island are the rapids known as Jeram Upeh Guling. In the granite boulders that form the bed of the river here are almost perfectly round holes, up to a metre across, like natural bath-tubs made out of the rock. Two to three hours trek further upstream, at Buaya

Sangkut, the river makes a fierce plunge. From limpid green pools in the terraced rock above the falls, it suddenly drops 15 metres (50 feet) in a rage of white water. In the early morning, a cloud hovers just above the waterfall where the spray gathers. Visitors to this lovely spot should take care when exploring close to the river.

At Buaya Sangkut, and on Gunung Janing, the unique fan-palm, *Livistona endauensis*, predominates in the surrounding forest. It is a most impressive sight, but there is little in a fan-palm forest that animals can eat. A few gibbons and monkeys may pass through but will not stay, and a group of pigs, here often the unusual Bearded Pig, may come to forage through the leaf litter.

Conservation and New Discoveries

Thanks to work by the Department of Wildlife and National Parks since the 1970s, and expeditions by the Malaysian Nature Society in 1985 and 1989, more is known about Endau Rompin than any other park in Peninsular Malaysia. Besides the discovery of new species, many aspects of forest ecology on shallow sandstone soils and of riverine biology have been studied.

The Johor sector is now managed by the National Parks Corporation (Johor). This body is specifically charged with the creation, management and maintenance of a network of areas for conservation, research, education and recreation.

The Pahang sector of the park, Rompin Endau, is usually reached via dirt roads from the coastal town of Pontian, leading north of the flat-topped mountain Gunung Keriong, to the Sungai Kinchin. There is more alluvial forest here than in the Johor sector, and it contains various trees that are confined to the southern part of Peninsular Malaysia, including the white-flowered *Dillenia albiflos*. A rare bird here is the Giant Pitta.

Above: *The unique fan-palm* Livistona endauensis *grows in shallow soils on the hilltops.*

Top right: *Black and white colouring is found in a number of mainly nocturnal mammals such as the Malayan Tapir.*

Centre right: *Sambar stags give an explosive steam-engine whistle if alarmed by visitors.*

Bottom right: *Endau Rompin is famous for its Sumatran Rhinoceros, a few of which are still left here.*

TAMAN NEGARA

Malaysia's First National Park

Taman Negara is home to one of the world's oldest tropical rain forests. Plant fossils almost identical with species existing now have been found in rock dating back 130 million years. Established by state legislation in 1938, this was Malaysia's first national park and is the largest, covering 4,343 square kilometres (1,680 square miles). The bulk of the park lies between 75 and 300 metres altitude (250–1,000 feet), fringing the central highland core that rises to the summit of Gunung Tahan, which at 2,187 metres (7,186 feet) is the highest peak in all of Peninsular Malaysia.

Biodiversity

The gently undulating country in the lowlands harbours almost all of the large mammals of Peninsular Malaysia. Most of them will remain invisible, but footprints of tigers, *seladang* (Gaur), pigs and deer are sometimes found along the walking trails. Elephants may leave evidence of their passage in the form of broken branches in the understorey.

Taman Negara may well contain all of the inland forest bird species that occur in the Peninsula. More than 300 have been counted, of which 292 are known to be dependent on forest for their survival. Another 54 bird

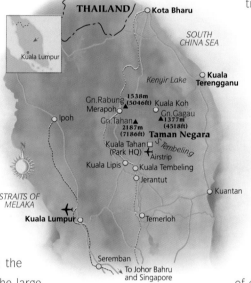

species are restricted in Taman Negara to highland forest, including two large rarities, the Mountain Peacock Pheasant and the Crested Argus Pheasant.

Though the lowland forest has the greatest variety of plants as well as animals, the highland forest has the most species with very confined distributions. The Tahan massif, for example, is the only known home of *Livistona tahanensis*, an elegant small fan-palm that is quite common there.

Treks and Trails

A walk is the best way to experience the park and its forests, whether it is wandering the well-marked trails around park headquarters at Kuala Tahan, or making longer treks to other areas. In the cool of dawn when birdlife is most active, in the humid sluggishness of midday or the darkness of night, the rain forest offers different impressions. The dense foliage and the retiring habits of the animals mean that most visitors will not at first see much wildlife apart from squirrels, birds and insects. But if one is very quiet, it will not be long before other inhabitants such as monkeys, gibbons and perhaps even a mousedeer will appear.

The 400-metre (1,300-foot) canopy walkway at Kuala Tahan, the longest such walkway in the world, gives birdwatchers many opportunities. Those seeking bigger animals, such as deer or tapir, may try their luck by staying overnight at a hide overlooking a salt lick or clearing, such as Yong Hide, Blau Hide or, best of all, Kumbang Hide. The self-discipline to keep very still is needed when

Opposite: The forest of Taman Negara helps to mitigate flooding along big rivers such as the Sungai Tembeling.

Above, right: A range of accommodation is available at the park, including the Taman Negara Resort.

Location: Over parts of Pahang, Kelantan and Terengganu; 59 km (37 miles) upriver from Kuala Tembeling 54 km/34 miles north of Temerloh on the Kuala Lumpur-to-Kuantan road.

Climate: 25°–37°C (77°–99°F). Typically hot and humid, but cool and sunny in mountains, cold on peaks at night. More rain October–February.

When to Go: March–September. Mid-November–mid-January not so good for walking and wildlife.

Access: Taxi or train to Kuala Tembeling on Singapore-to-Kota Bharu line. Or bus to Jerantut then taxi to Tembeling. Boat up the Sungai Tembeling to park HQ. Drive or fly to a point near Kuala Tahan. Alternative access via Kelantan and Terengganu.

Permits: Book park boats and accommodation with Taman Negara Resort office in Kuala Lumpur(or other operators), ask at Kuala Tahan. Entry, camera and fishing fees paid at park HQ.

Equipment: Camping, hiking and fishing equipment for hire. Torch for night walks. Light clothes for forest walks, warm clothes for climbing; hiking boots (sleeping bag for long hikes).

Facilities: Reception and information centre, chalets, camping area, restaurants, shop. Three visitors' lodges, two fishing lodges. Hides, canopy walkways.

Wildlife: Birds, bats, snakes. Elephants, bears and other big mammals possible.

Visitor Activities: Walking, trekking, river trips, swimming.

you are on lookout. Large animals may not come every night but these hides are the best, though not guaranteed, means of seeing them.

Guides are required for longer treks, which include interesting trips to some of the limestone caves found in Taman Negara. The most often visited cave is Gua Telinga, less than an hour's walk south of Kuala Tahan. Gua Daun Menari is larger, with more bats, accessible from Kuala Keniyam. Gua Besar is a limestone massif still deeper into the forest, but with few caves. Gua Peningat, highest limestone peak in the peninsula at 714 metres (2,340 feet), is reached via the western access point of Merapoh, and energetic visitors can scramble all the way up to the top.

Climbing Gunung Tahan

Those with more time can attempt the ascent of Gunung Tahan. At least seven days of trekking are needed to cover the 55 kilometres (35 miles) from Kuala Tahan and back again. The second day is the most gruelling, and involves a climb up and down 21 hills. On the third day the climb of the mountain really begins, part of it on all fours up earth banks, before emerging at mid-mountain altitude at Wray's Camp. The last day includes a scramble up steep quartzite, and ends at the famous *padang* of low, open scrub just below the true peak. Here you may see the Hill Prinia, a small warbler-like bird for which the *padang* is its only home between northern Thailand and Sumatra. An ascent from Merapoh can shorten the trek to three days.

Rivers and Rapids

A less strenuous but more expensive way to explore the natural features of Taman Negara is to hire a boat for a trip along one of the park's many rivers and tributaries. These include a scenic ride to the rapids of Lata Berkoh and a journey through

Above: Fungi are little studied but of huge importance in nutrient cycling within the forest.

Right: Leaf-insects, magnificently coloured to resemble growing leaves, are active mainly by night.

Far right: Each red lobe of the ginger inflorescence represents one flower.

Below, right: Water monitors can be seen by most visitors along the rivers or even at the headquarters of the park.

Opposite, left: Aboriginal peoples, though they have carefully defined rights within the park, now depend little upon hunting.

Opposite, right: Taman Negara has the longest canopy walkway anywhere in the world.

the whitewater rapids of the Sungai Tembeling. Boat trips can also shorten the treks to some of the less accessible places within the park, which include Kuala Terengan and Kuala Keniyam and the wildlife observation hides.

Access and Accommodation

Taman Negara now has four access points: Kuala Tahan and Merapoh in Pahang, Kuala Koh in Kelantan, and Tanjung Mentong in Terengganu. Kuala Tahan, the traditional entry point into the park, is accessible by boat (a three hour ride) from Kuala Tembeling near Jerantut in Pahang; or by air from Kuala Lumpur and Singapore. Merapoh can be reached by ordinary car or by train, Kuala Koh by four-wheel drive along jeep tracks through the oil-palm plantations. Access to the newest visitor centre at Tanjung Mentong, in Terengganu, is only by boat across Kenyir lake. This centre is notable for two features: it is within reach of the limestone hills Gua Bidan and Gua Taat, and also offers the possibility of a trek to the little-known mountain Gunung Gagau. Accommodation within the park includes a hostel, chalets and campsites.

Above, top: *The ascent of Gunung Tahan, the Peninsula's highest mountain, involves a trek of several days.*

Above, centre: *Fishing is permitted in certain areas, but only with a licence.*

Above, bottom: *The challenge of the rapids alters from day to day, depending on water levels.*

Right: *Trees arching over the smaller rivers are a special feature of the lowland forest here.*

BAKO NATIONAL PARK

Sarawak's First National Park

Bako was the first national park to be established in Sarawak, in 1957, and is still a showpiece in the system of protected areas. Covering about 27 square kilometres (10 square miles) of forest, it occupies a mainly sandstone peninsula on the South China Sea opposite Gunung Santubong. Its attraction is due partly to the wide variety of forest types within this small area, and partly to the impressive seascapes and rockscapes along the coast.

Characteristic Plants

Much of Bako National Park is on thin, white, sandy soils that lie over level sandstone plateaux at different levels above the sea. In places, peat builds up, forming a thin, dark layer, with lots of tree roots but it is easily eroded or dislodged. This makes for

Opposite, top: Seen from the beach at Bako, the legend-shrouded Gunung Santubong dominates the impressive view across the bay.

Opposite, bottom left: The monkey most likely to be seen at Bako is the Long-tailed Macaque, especially near the park headquarters where it searches for scraps of food.

Opposite, bottom right: The flying lemur or Colugo is nocturnal, glides from tree to tree rather than flies, and is well camouflaged when at rest.

Above, right: The squat pitchers of Nepenthes rafflesiana *growing near ground level are distinct from the slender ones higher up the same plant.*

a very nutrient-poor environment. Pitcher plants, ant plants and sundews are characteristic of the forest, as all these plants are able to acquire some nutrients from sources other than the soil. One of the most common pitcher plants at Bako is *Nepenthes ampullaria*, which is typically restricted to the ground. This is a species with fat round pitchers with slender lids. Insects perching on the slippery rim tend to fall into the soupy water inside, where they die and are digested. Sundews have leaves with sticky tips, which trap any unfortunate victim that settles on them.

The entire forest reflects the low nutrient status of the soils. Stunted trees grow (especially on the exposed plateaux and where the sands form only a thin layer over the bedrock) with roots that hardly penetrate below the surface. It is easy to see the differences between forest growth in different parts of the park: along the coast, on the higher ground, and within the smaller valleys. Most distinctive is the patchy growth of mangroves in sheltered areas where sediment gathers. A good stand of mangroves awaits arriving visitors at Teluk Assam where the boats reach the jetty. The next bay south, Teluk Delima, also has some mangroves; here, these are mixed with clumps of the extremely spiny nibong palm.

Wildlife Experiences

It is usually difficult to find big animals in Sarawak's parks because of the impact of former hunting, but Bako is the exception. The impressive Bearded Pig can often be seen foraging in the forest close to the park head-

Location: About 40 km (25 miles) northeast of Kuching, the state capital, on a sandstone headland on the coast.

Climate: Hot by day, moderate by night. It is generally pleasant within the forest, but can be very hot in open sandy areas on the sandstone headland plateau.

When to Go: A good wildlife experience at any time of year; more migrant birds between September and March.

Access: Easily accessible by bus (or taxi) from Kuching to Kampung Bako, then by small boat to the park headquarters at Teluk Assam. Rough seas can prevent exit in afternoons, November–February.

Permits: Easily arranged at the office at Kampung Bako, where boats depart for the park. Accommodation must be booked in advance through the National Parks and Wildlife Office in Kuching.

Equipment: Light clothing, good walking shoes; swimwear and sunblock. Insect repellent handy in the evenings.

Facilities: Information office, jetty, simple chalets and hostels and canteen. Trails through park.

Wildlife: Bearded Pigs and Long-tailed Macaques usually seen around park HQ. Do not feed the monkeys. Proboscis Monkeys occasionally give good sightings.

Visitor Activities: Walking, wildlife, plants. Snorkelling around Pulau Lakei and Teluk Limau 8 km (5 miles) northeast of park HQ. Coast good for photography.

quarters, or behind the canteen. These tall, rangy-looking pigs are an important food source in Borneo. Both sexes sport great clumps of blond whiskers either side of the jaw. Their teeth are massive – much heavier than those of the Peninsular Malaysian wild boar – and are probably adapted to crushing tough, fibrous roots, tubers, and the hard seeds of forest fruits.

The visitor looking for Proboscis Monkeys may be lucky enough to find them anywhere in the taller forest, but they are most likely to be seen in one of the mangrove patches, perhaps at Teluk Delima, the next bay south from Teluk Assam. An encounter between groups, with two big males honking and displaying at each other, and their attendant females milling around, is an impressive and exciting sight. These monkeys are among the few mammals that appear to be at home in the nibong palms, and can land with a thump upon a spine-riddled palm trunk, unharmed and oblivious to the formidable thorns.

About 150 species of birds have been found at Bako, a moderate total. It is one of the few places where a selection of waders, seabirds and forest birds can be found together. Between September and March there are usually a few Lesser Golden Plovers, Whimbrels or Curlew Sandpipers about. In the mangroves, look out for birds such as the Copper-throated Sunbird and the Mangrove Flycatcher. Seabirds occasionally pass by; a Red-footed Booby was recently recorded. Furthermore Bako, being on a peninsula picks up a number of migrants such as Yellow Wagtails, Grey Wagtails, and a few rarities. The variety of birds is therefore better during the northern autumn and spring, when migration by waders and passerines is under way.

Exploration

Bako has a number of good, well-marked visitor trails (and maps at all junctions). One leads from the park headquarters south to Teluk Delima less than an hour away. The Lintang trail is a 5-kilometre (3-mile) loop through a variety of forest types, extending over the sandstone plateau but beginning and ending in better forest near the sea. It is also good to explore the coastline where, north of Teluk Assam in particular, wave action has sculpted the richly coloured rock into strange shapes.

For those interested in park management, Bako makes a good study. Visitor access is by boat, from the village of Kampung Bako across the bay, and is therefore highly controllable. Bako is extremely popular, with many tour parties arriving from Kuching, and is usually at its busiest from about June to August. To lessen the impact on the environment, some trails are periodically closed so the ground and vegetation on the fragile white sands of the plateau areas can recover.

Below: *Male fiddler crabs, with one big claw, have brilliant colours that differ from species to species.*

Above: *The accessibility of Bako National Park makes it an ideal location for local naturalists and school parties to visit.*

Far left: *The tide inundates the breathing roots of mangrove trees close to park headquarters.*

Left: *Richly coloured sandstone is characteristic of Bako's coastline.*

GUNUNG MULU NATIONAL PARK

Sarawak's Largest Park

The biggest and arguably the most spectacular of Sarawak's parks is Gunung Mulu National Park. Located in the northeast of the state, in Miri and Limbang Divisions, its 528 square kilometres (204 square miles) lie just south of the international border with Brunei Darussalam.

Steep, rugged limestone mountains and deep gorges run through the heart of the park. The Melinau Gorge and its river separate the peak of Gunung Api (1,750 metres/5,740 feet), with its astonishing limestone pinnacles, from that of Gunung Benarat before the river continues at a leisurely pace through the lowlands of the park. Further east, the more rounded sandstone peak of Gunung Mulu, first climbed in 1932, rises to 2,376 metres (7,796 feet).

The Caves

The outstanding limestone formations and caves have made Gunung Mulu internationally famous. Superlatives used to describe the caves include the biggest natural chamber in the world (the Sarawak Chamber, a vast unsupported dome); the largest cave passage known in the world (the Deer Cave); and the longest cave system in Southeast Asia (Clearwater Cave), in which over 100

Opposite: *The Sungai Melinau provides an atmospheric approach to Gunung Mulu National Park from the visitor accommodation downstream.*

Above, right: *Long, narrow boats for the use of visitors regularly ply the park's river system.*

kilometres (62 miles) of passages have been discovered and more may yet be found. These last two, and another two show-caves known as Wind Cave and Lang's Cave, are open to visitors.

One sight that all visitors hope to witness is the tremendous display of bats emerging from the Deer Cave. This can vary enormously depending on the weather, but on the best evenings more than a million bats fly out in successive waves, taking more than an hour and a half to emerge. These are virtually all Wrinkle-lipped Bats, the other species in the cave leaving separately in small numbers. As the bats depart to feed over the surrounding forest, Bat Hawks and Peregrine Falcons take the chance to snatch a meal on the wing.

The Gunung Mulu Trail and the Pinnacles

The trek to Gunung Mulu's summit takes several days, starting with a long walk through lowland forest to the first camp at the base of the mountain. The climb itself usually takes another two days, ending at Camp 4 just below the summit. A further two days are needed to return all the way to park headquarters. In the summit zone, passing from lower montane forest into mossy ericaceous forest with rhododendrons and trees festooned with lichens, the trek occasionally involves scrambling up a wet moss-covered bank or holding onto tree roots, but is seldom seriously difficult.

The Pinnacles of Gunung Api are one of the park's most outstanding features. Created by the eroding

Location: In eastern Sarawak, about 100 km (60 miles) in a straight line southeast of Miri.

Climate: Hot by day, warm by night. Forest more equable; nights cold nights on mountain. Rain at any time, but wetter October– February.

When to Go: Any time, but wet weather makes activities trying.

Access: From Miri either by air to Gunung Mulu (regular daily flights), or by river from Kuala Baram (the port outside Miri) to Marudi and Long Terawan, then by boat to the park.

Permits: Arranged with National Parks and Wildlife Office in Miri or Kuching. Tour operators make arrangements for clients; other travellers must get permits and book accommodation in advance.

Equipment: Light clothes and strong shoes or boots with good grip needed for forest walking and caves; strong torch useful. Specialist cavers should bring their own equipment.

Facilities: Park HQ, information centre, chalets and canteen. Camping at designated points (e.g. summit trail). Boat services and guides. Boardwalk to Deer Cave, trail system. Four caves with lighting and walkways; specialist caving available.

Wildlife: Birdwatching and bat-watching with Bat Hawks and sometimes Peregrines.

Visitor Activities: Visiting caves. Caving, climbing, forest walks, birdwatching, photography. Trek to Gunung Mulu peak and limestone Pinnacles.

Above: *A small community of Penan people lives close to the park. Here a Penan woman treads sago in the traditional way.*

action of water on limestone, these razor-edged stones protrude vertically from the stunted forest around their bases. Although limestone features of similar shape can be found in other parts of the country, none is so big as these; the Pinnacles reach over 60 metres (200 feet). Most are clustered on one limestone slope, and can best be seen either from the air or from the top point of the climb from Camp 5 (in the Melinau Gorge), which is about a three-hour walk.

As part of the park's management strategy, no trail maps are provided and all visitors must be accompanied by a recognized guide. Those going on the longer treks have to be accompanied by a park ranger.

Hornbills

It is difficult to find large animals in the park, but hornbills can be seen and heard, especially on the treks to Camp 5 or to the summit of Gunung Mulu. A retching sound coming from the middle storey of the forest may reveal a pair of Black Hornbills, or a barking noise may herald the take-off of a small group of Wreathed Hornbills from the forest canopy. Bushy-crested Hornbills live in extended family groups with several generations of grown young, and make a high-pitched yelping like a group of puppies.

Plant Life

The park's forests remain largely undisturbed and comprise a complex of mixed dipterocarp forest, peat swamp, forest over limestone, and montane forests. The plant life is of great importance. Along the 3-kilometre (2-mile) boardwalk leading to Deer Cave is a range of lowland forest, some of it growing on swampy, seasonally flooded ground. The rare *Cryptocoryne*, a little aquatic plant producing flowers like a miniature Arum Lily, grows in the ever-wet spots, while interesting limestone specialists grow closer to the caves. The climb to the Pinnacles is particularly rewarding to botanists. Pink-blossomed balsams, the flasks of pitcher plants, and an outstanding array of species of the One-leafed Plant group *Monophyllea* can be observed along the way.

The drama of Gunung Mulu: rugged limestone hills (above); *bats emerging from the Deer Cave* (right); *Wind Cave rock formations* (far right, above); *the grandeur of Clearwater Cave* (opposite, left); *undisturbed plant life* (far right, below).

Local Communities

The local communities living around the park include Penan, Berawan, Lun Bawang and Iban people. The inhabitants of certain longhouses are allowed to continue to hunt pigs and deer, to fish, and to collect forest produce for food or handicrafts in specified areas of the park. Some of the Penan live in a permanent longhouse at Batu Bungan, immediately outside the park boundary. This has been incorporated into some tourists' itineraries on the way to or from Clearwater and Wind Caves. Remember to take off your muddy boots, before climbing the steps to look at some of the handicrafts such as baskets and bracelets.

Research at Gunung Mulu

Gunung Mulu National Park is being strongly promoted by the governmental and private sectors but many of its resources remain little known. Since the first big expedition by the Royal Geographical Society and the Sarawak State Government in 1977–78, international teams of scientists and explorers have visited the park but their expeditions have mostly concentrated on the caves.

Right: *The great height of the razor-sharp Pinnacles is revealed by the adjacent trees.*

Overleaf: *The Deer Cave is the biggest cave passage in the world, and is home to over a million bats.*

KINABALU PARK

Malaysia's Highest Mountain

Kinabalu Park was established in 1964, and protects 754 square kilometres (291 square miles) of extremely diverse country, from lowland forest up to bare granite peaks. The park's outstanding feature is Gunung Kinabalu, the highest mountain in Malaysia, reaching 4,095 metres (13,436 feet) at Low's Peak, one of several peaks of similar altitude in the summit zone.

Gunung Kinabalu is still rising imperceptibly, and broods over the landscape of Sabah; in clear weather it is visible from an enormous area of the state. At about 3,900 metres (12,800 feet) a rocky crescent, with two arms known as the western and eastern plateaux, embraces Low's Gully, a precipitous-sided black hole that is over a kilometre (nearly a mile) deep in some places.

Opposite, top left: *The shiny, deep purple orchid* Bulbophyllum vinaceum *seldom has more than a single waxy blossom on any one plant.*

Opposite, centre left: *Birdwatchers along the trails are likely to see montane specialists such as the Indigo Flycatcher.*

Opposite, bottom left: *Kinabalu Park is prized for its rhododendrons, such as* Rhododendron rugosum, *which are zoned at different altitudes up the mountain.*

Opposite, right: *In the montane forest, the trees are gnarled and there is a profusion of mosses and epiphytes that thrive in the damp conditions.*

Above, right: *The dramatic profile of Gunung Kinabalu is characterized by the Donkey's Ears, two granite pinnacles.*

Rich Flora

Kinabalu Park has one of the greatest concentrations of plant species on earth, largely because of the mountain which provides such a range of habitats at different altitudes. It is estimated that over 4,500 species occur here, including about 1,500 orchids, of which 77 are endemic to the park. There are more species of rhododendrons and pitcher plants here than in any similar-sized area. The Rajah Pitcher Plant has the biggest known pitcher of any, up to 2 litres (3½ pints) in capacity, while one of the most elegant is the flask-shaped Low's Pitcher Plant.

Mixed dipterocarp forest dominates most lowland areas and is extremely rich in tree species. From 1,200 metres (4,000 feet) up to 2,350 metres (7,700 feet), lower montane forest grows. Species of oaks, laurels, myrtles, conifers and members of the tea family are among the commoner trees. Higher still, upper montane forest reaches 3,000 metres (9,800 feet), characterized on Gunung Kinabalu by magnificent rhododendrons. Increasingly with altitude the forest becomes moss-covered, gnarled and stunted, until the tree line is reached between 3,350 metres (11,000 feet) and 3,700 metres (12,100 feet). The highest vegetation of all is known as subalpine vegetation, and Gunung Kinabalu is the only Malaysian mountain high enough to support it. Above this, there is no soil on the steep, smooth rocks.

Animal Life

Kinabalu Park's animal life is as outstanding as its flora and includes 289 species of birds, with specialities like

Location: 60 km (37 miles) northeast of Kota Kinabalu.

Climate: Hot and humid in the lowlands (28°C/82°F), and very cold at the summit of Gunung Kinabalu (6°–8°C/42°–46°F).

When to Go: Any time of year, perhaps best in March, with usually clear skies and little rain. If possible avoid wetter months around November–February.

Access: Bus or taxi from Kota Kinabalu in about 2 hours; the new Mesilau visitor centre is 5 km (3 miles) further on. About another hour to the lowlands visitor centre at Poring.

Permits: Only required for climbing Gunung Kinabalu. Small charge for vehicle access.

Equipment: In the lowlands and headquarters, light forest wear and walking boots, with a pullover or jacket in evening. Mountain climbers should take waterproof jacket, warm clothing.

Facilities: Information centre, bookshop, restaurants. Book accommodation well in advance, through Sabah Parks office in Kota Kinabalu. Various trails near headquarters. Single trail to summit on mountain, rest stops, overnight accommodation and restaurant at Panar Laban at 3,300 m (10,850 ft). At Poring, hot springs, baths; canopy walkway.

Wildlife: Magnificent birdwatching opportunities. For botanists, a vast array of plants with many endemics.

Visitor Activities: Bird and plant spotting, walking forest trails, climbing the peak; photography.

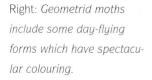

Above: *At lowland Poring, hot spring baths are popular with weekend visitors.*

the Kinabalu Serpent-eagle and Kinabalu Friendly Warbler, Crimson-breasted Wood Partridge and Bornean Mountain Whistler. Not many are confined to Gunung Kinabalu, but they are particularly easy to see in the environment provided around the park headquarters. There are at least 290 species of butterflies, 100 species of reptiles, 40 species of freshwater fish, and an unknown but vast assemblage of invertebrates still being studied.

Trekking and Climbing

Around the headquarters at 1,500 metres (5,000 feet) there are several forest trails to explore. There are three mountain ascent routes: the Summit Trail is the one used by all ordinary visitors and tourists, while Kotal's Trail and Bowen's Trail require special permission and, for the latter, rock-climbing experience. Never forget the potential dangers on the mountain.

The trek to Low's Peak takes two days, beginning with an uphill climb all the way to Panar Laban at 3,300 metres (11,000 feet) where there is overnight accommodation. Most climbers begin the final ascent at 3 am the next morning, in order to reach the peak at sunrise. The vast landscapes over lowland Sabah, with the sight of the mountain's shadow edging across the clouds, are an indescribable experience. It is then possible to climb all the way down to park headquarters on the same day.

Poring Hot Springs lie 43 kilometres (27 miles) to the southeast. There are five hot springs with bathing facilities, several forest trails leading to waterfalls and caves, and a canopy walkway. Near the foot of the walkway, *Rafflesia* is sometimes in flower. The walkway itself is good for birdwatching, looking for canopy insects, and viewing the crowns of the biggest trees.

Map labels:
Low's Peak
Oyayubi Iwu Peak ▲ ▲ Ugly Sister Peak King Edward Peak
St.Johns Peak ▲ ▲ Donkey Ears Peak
▲ Tunku Abdul Rahman
South Peak ▲
Sayat-Sayat hut
Panar Laban hut
Laban Rata hut
Kota Kinabalu
Paka cave shelter
Villosa shelter
Layang-Layang hut
Kamborongon Telecom Station ●
Mempening shelter
Lowii shelter
Ubah shelter
Kandi shelter
Park HQ
Timpohon Gate
N

Right: *Geometrid moths include some day-flying forms which have spectacular colouring.*

Far right: *One of Borneo's 33 endemic birds is the spectacular but rarely seen Whitehead's Trogon.*

Right and far right: *Kinabalu is famous for its orchids; some 1,500 species occur here. Renanthera bella* (right) *grows only where the soil is mineral rich. Bulbophyllum lobbii (far right), a small orchid species, grows close to ground level.*

Achievements at Kinabalu Park

Kinabalu is an important research site, currently conducting a major study on ethnobotany. There is a montane plant garden which doubles as an exhibit and an opportunity for study. The park also has laboratories, a herbarium, a museum collection and, at headquarters, educational facilities for visitors.

Surrounding the park are areas cultivated by Kadazan Dusun peoples, Sabah's largest community of indigenous residents. Many members of the local community work in the park as rangers and guides, so that the park is able to bring an economic benefit to the surrounding villages. Further benefits flow from the sale of foodstuffs, especially fruit and vegetables, and opportunities to work in the increasing number of hotels.

Right: *Steps help along some stretches of the invariably steep and long ascent of Gunung Kinabalu.*

Below: *One of the most oddly shaped pitcher plants is* Nepenthes lowii, *which grows at mid-mountain altitudes*

Above, top: *St John's Peak on Gunung Kinabalu shows clear evidence of glacial action in the geological past.*

Above, centre: *An early morning climb to the peak allows plenty of time for a careful descent, following the safety ropes, before the sun gets too hot.*

Above, bottom: *Gunung Kinabalu's massive summit scenery forms a great contrast with the richly forested lowlands below; up here even lichens are scarce.*

Right: *Seen from the agricultural area of Kundasan, Gunung Kinabalu dominates the skyline.*

KABILI-SEPILOK FOREST RESERVE

Orang-utan Rehabilitation in the Forest

The Kabili-Sepilok Forest Reserve is one of the most important surviving remnants of Sabah's once rich and extensive forested areas. Occupying an area of 43 square kilometres (16 square miles), the reserve is covered almost entirely by lowland forests in which timber trees of the family Dipterocarpaceae predominate both in numbers and in size.

Orang-utans

The Orang-utan Rehabilitation Centre is by far the best known facility in Sepilok and the work here has attracted much attention world wide. The centre was established in 1964 by the Sabah Wildlife Department (at that time a part of the Forestry Department), and aimed to facilitate the rehabilitation of Orang-utans confiscated from captivity or displaced by forest clearance. Visitors are allowed to interact with the Orang-utans at feeding times, which occur twice a day. The animals are viewed at specially built feeding platforms from boardwalks above the forest floor, so as to minimize the impact of visitor numbers.

The Mangrove Trail

Although most visitors to Sepilok do not venture away from the boardwalks, there are several forest trails that

Opposite, right: The mixed dipterocarp forest at Kabili-Sepilok is rich in species and provides structural complexity for the animals to move within.

Above, right: Massive adult male Orang-utans typically stay at ground level.

are worth exploring. One of the most accessible is the mangrove trail, which runs from the Rehabilitation Centre and leads over sandstone ridges into the mangrove forests on the boundary of the reserve. Here, a small reception centre has been set up with basic accommodation facilities.

The trail begins in the low-lying area of the reserve, where flat land supports forests that are seasonally flooded by rain and the floodwater from nearby streams. Here, the Borneo Ironwood is found. These large timber trees, sought after for centuries for their durable wood, are found only in Borneo and the Philippines, and today very few examples exist outside forest reserves. Another rare plant is a small terrestrial orchid, *Cymbidium borneense*, known only from the reserve.

Leading away from the flat ground, the trail begins to ascend the sandstone ridges which dominate the reserve. Different tree species make up the forest here, with large canopy trees (such as *Parashorea tomentella*, which are common in the lowlands) being replaced by *Shorea multiflora* and *Dipterocarpus acutangulus*. This is the most challenging part of the trail, leading across the undulating hills, but the air here is not so densely humid as in the lower-lying areas of the reserve.

On the descent, the lofty forest begins to lose its stature as it leads into first the fringes and then the main expanse of the mangrove swamp, where the trees grow in deep mud and need specialized roots both to anchor and to breathe. Proboscis Monkeys occur here, and feed almost entirely on the mangrove foliage. The trail ends at the reception centre of Sepilok Laut.

Another way to visit the mangroves is by speedboat

Map labels:
To Ranau
To Sandakan
Kota Kinabalu
Kabili-Sepilok Forest Reserve
Car Park
Visitor Centre
Feeding Platform
Education Centre
Feeding Platform
Nature Ridge Trail
Ridge
Mangroves
Sandakan Bay

Location: 24 km (15 miles) by road from Sandakan town, and 11 km (7 miles) from Sandakan airport, in eastern Sabah.

Climate: Usually warm by day inside the forest, hotter out in the open, with more likelihood of rain in the afternoon and evening. Wetter weather is more likely from October– February.

When to Go: Any time of year. The centre is open from 9 am–4 pm daily; Orang-utans usually fed about 9.30 or 10 am and 2.30 pm.

Access: By bus, four times daily from Sandakan bus station, or by taxi. You can arrange with a taxi driver for your return.

Permits: Not needed in advance. Entrance charge for visitors. If you intend to walk the mangrove trail or visit by boat, permission is required from Sabah Forestry Department, which is close to Sepilok outside Sandakan.

Equipment: Light clothing and footwear, stronger boots useful for walking forest trails .

Facilities: Reception area, restaurant, exhibits, trails, boardwalk to the Orang-utan feeding area. Overnight accommodation in various hotels in Sandakan town.

Wildlife: Mainly Orang-utans, but 277 species of birds have been recorded, and there is a range of other lowland forest animals and plants.

Visitor Activities: Orang-utan watching and photography. Do not feed the animals and do not carry food with you. Trail walking. Boat trips to the mangroves.

Right, top left: *The long-term programme at Kabili-Sepilok has permitted ithe monitoring of individual Orang-utans over long periods.*

Right, top right: *Health is an important criterion in judging whether a rehabilitant Orang-utan is ready to take its first steps into the forest.*

Right, centre: *Troops of Pig-tailed Macaques clear up scraps from the feeding platform after the rehabilitant Orang-utans have had their fill in the morning.*

Right, bottom left: *Like any infants, Orang-utans benefit from care and attention while learning how to cope with their environment.*

Opposite: *Carefully designed boardwalks reduce visitor impact upon the forest, while allowing close and detailed views of plant and animal life.*

from Sandakan. Yet another alternative is to come into the mangroves by boat, and walk out along the trail over the ridges.

Forest Resources

About 2 kilometres (1½ miles) away from the Rehabilitation Centre the Rainforest Interpretation Centre is well worth a visit. From here, a short well-labelled nature trail runs through the arboretum belonging to the Forest Research Centre. Information boards have been erected at selected points to highlight various features of the vegetation.

Specialists who visit Sepilok are still discovering new plant species among its botanical wealth. Recently, a local botanist discovered two new species of palms that can be found only within the reserve. The forest plants also have the potential to supply new drugs and medicines. As a source of seed material for the enrichment of other forested areas, or for the development of forest plantations, the reserve remains a living gene bank of resources. It is also of special interest as a place where inland forest remains continuous down to the coast.

SUNGAI KINABATANGAN

Along Sabah's Longest River

The Kinabatangan Wildlife Sanctuary lies within the vast floodplain of the Sungai Kinabatangan – one of the longest rivers in Malaysia. At 270 square kilometres (104 square miles), the sanctuary is part of an important network of conservation areas in the lowlands of eastern Sabah, together forming a corridor of natural vegetation which links the lower, tidal, mangrove-fringed reaches of the river to the seemingly limitless inland forests of the upper catchment area and its hills.

Lowland Diversity

The Sungai Kinabatangan begins its course deep in the forested interior of Sabah. Where the river reaches the lowlands, a rich mosaic of forests, swamps and limestone outcrops covers one of Malaysia's largest floodplains. In areas where the land remains under water for long periods, the forests give way to open woodlands or to herbaceous swamps that are sometimes almost entirely carpeted with sedges and grasses. Oxbow lakes, formed by large meanders of the river that have been cut off from the main channel, are a common feature.

It is not surprising, given these varied habitats, that there is a bewildering abundance and diversity of wildlife. Among the primates that share the forest are Orang-utans, and during the drier months of the year Asian Elephants, one of the region's most highly endangered species, roam here on their annual migration to the floodplain. In the network of rivers, swamps and lakes many aquatic animals can be found including bony fish, freshwater rays and sharks, and crocodiles. A recent study of the sharks rediscovered a freshwater species that had not seen during the previous eight decades.

A River Safari

The best way to experience the beauty of Sungai Kinabatangan is by river safari. Village boats, or tourist boats operated by established companies, are available to visitors at some of the riverside villages such as Sukau and Batu Putih. The most magical moments are at dawn, when the chorus of birds and the bubbling calls of the gibbons give a very clear impression of the forest waking up for the day ahead. Often one can hear the unmistakable sound of hornbills in flight, their stiff wing feathers sighing at every beat. Sometimes the more enigmatic of Kinabatangan's inhabitants can be glimpsed: otters at play, or Orang-utans moving slowly and languidly through the forest.

At dusk, Proboscis Monkeys begin to gather along the riverine forest margins. These charismatic primates – the males distinguished by their huge, pendulous red noses – seem relatively undisturbed by humans when they begin to settle to sleep, and are fascinating to watch at close quarters in the fading light.

The Gomantong Caves

The Gomantong Caves lie about 10 kilometres (6 miles) from the visitor lodges at Sukau, and are easily accessible by road. They are within a forest reserve and therefore managed by the Forest Department, though

Opposite: *Upriver from where most of the visitor accommodation is located, there is access to a series of oxbow lakes, where crocodiles are known.*

Above right: *A serene atmosphere prevails as evening falls over the impressive Sungai Kinabatangan.*

Location: A huge river whose basin occupies much of eastern Sabah, with the estuary on the northern side of Dent Peninsula.

Climate: Lowland areas hot and humid by day, pleasantly cool by night. Wet weather more likely between October and February when there is some flooding of forested areas.

When to Go: Any time, but access more difficult when wet.

Access: By road (preferably 4-wheel drive) from Sandakan, circuitously west then south then east to Gomantong Caves, to reach the commonest access point at Sukau. Sukau is about 32 km (20 miles) from the estuary, and some tour companies prefer to take clients from Sandakan by boat along the coast and upriver.

Equipment: Light clothing for boat journeys and forest walking, with strong footwear that can survive frequent wetting. Torch for visiting caves and for night walks.

Facilities: Private companies operate tourist lodges at Sukau. They offer full board, boat services and trips to oxbow lakes and Gomantong Caves.

Wildlife: Proboscis Monkeys and other primates, lowland birds, hornbills, and raptors. Lucky visitors may see elephants.

Visitor Activities: Wildlife, river trips, forest walks, visits to oxbow lakes and caves. Evening boat trips to see Proboscis Monkeys (choose boats with silent electric motors). Look out for Oriental Darter and Storm's Stork.

day-to-day management also relies on the Sabah Wildlife Department because these caves are famous for their swiftlets and bird-nest collecting. In other caves, collectors climb long poles from the ground to reach the nests in the roof but at Gomantong the method is different – from the village on top of the limestone outcrop the collectors descend to the cave through potholes. The price of edible nests is tremendous, reaching several thousand dollars per kilogram, which encourages the collectors to take risks.

Visitors to the caves will become immediately aware of a very strong smell of ammonia which emanates from the vast amount of guano deposited by both swiftlets and bats. This guano, rich in nutrients, is in itself a micro-habitat for millions of invertebrates. The whole mass seethes with cockroaches and crickets.

Above: *Upriver from where most of the visitor accommodation is located, there is access to a series of oxbow lakes, where crocodiles are known.*

Below left: *By boat, will afford the closest and most rewarding encounter. The best site in the area for Proboscis Monkey watching is the Sungai Menanggul.*

Below: *Towards dusk, troops of Proboscis Monkeys begin to gather in riverside trees to prepare for sleep. This is often the best time to observe Borneo's most distinctive monkey, a tributary of the Kinabatangan.*

Conservation of the Floodplain

Since the early days of trade in Borneo, the Kinabatangan has been one of the major routes for access to the natural resources of the forest: rattans and resins from the trees, and edible birds' nests from the Gomantong Caves have been a few of the valued harvests of the area. The region also provides a constant supply of fresh water and a bounty of fish. Where such resources were near at hand, the Orang Sungai (a broad term applied to the people who settled along the rivers) established their small communities, and over centuries both forest and river have been central to their livelihood. Today, efforts are under way to encourage villagers' participation in tourism.

Working to maintain the balance between the wise use and protection of the floodplain has been the aim of conservation efforts. A partnership will have to be forged that not only includes government and the private sector but also the local people, on whom any developments will have a large impact.

Left above: *An innovative ladder system enables nest collectors at the Gomantong Caves to harvest swiftlet nests from the cave roof.*

Below right: *The much sought-after edible nests are then sorted on the communal verandah.*

SIPADAN AND THE SEMPORNA ISLANDS

Malaysia's Premier Dive Sites

The most southwesterly big peninsula in Sabah, the Dent Peninsula, is surrounded by a cluster of islands. The area is remote and wild. Sipadan, a tiny island, has been protected since 1933, but more recent proposals for marine protection are still being refined.

Pulau Sipadan

Pulau Sipadan is Malaysia's only island situated beyond the continental shelf, in oceanic waters, and rises from a depth of over 600 metres (2,000 feet). Extending over 16.4 hectares (40½ acres), it has attractive white sandy beaches but little natural vegetation left: many visitor huts cater for the needs of divers from all over the world. The island's spectacular coral reefs teem with a rich variety of marine life.

From Semporna, the nearest mainland town, a fast boat takes about an hour. The most interesting sight on the way is the occasional water village perched above the coral reefs (though these are not good for the corals).

Opposite, top left: *Pulau Sipadan's abundant reef life ranges from large barrel sponges to minute colourful fish.*

Opposite, centre left: *Bigeye Trevallies are one of several fish species that form large circling shoals.*

Opposite, bottom left: *Sipadan is outstanding in enabling divers to swim with large numbers of Green Turtles.*

Opposite, right: *The coral gardens here form part of an underwater paradise that deserves protection forever.*

Above, right: *The narrow, white-sand shore of Pulau Sipadan is shaded by elegant windswept palms.*

Sipadan is the country's premier diving site, and one of the best in the world. The most spectacular sight is the drop-off zone at the edge of the reef, which is characterized by vertical or overhanging rock faces and in some places goes down to 600 metres (2,000 feet). Most of the dive sites have been given names such as Barracuda Point, Coral Gardens, Turtle Patch and Staghorn Crest; all of these are well-known snorkelling and diving spots.

The reef rim, which lies just beyond the crest of the reef, is the most actively growing area for corals. The smaller fish to be seen in this part include butterflyfish, damselfish and groupers. There are also medium-sized to large open water species such as snappers and surgeonfish. Whitetip Reef Sharks, turtles and manta rays visit the area.

One cave in the reef wall acts as a trap for unwary turtles, which occasionally die there; bones or skulls can still be seen. Some turtles still nest on the beaches of Sipadan, and you may be lucky enough to see one of the very few remaining Coconut Crabs. The island has been a bird sanctuary for many years, administered by the Sabah Wildlife Department; apart from Pied Imperial Pigeons and a few other species, a bird to look out for is the White-throated Mangrove Whistler, a Philippine bird with a foothold here in Borneo.

The Semporna Islands

About 50 kilometres (30 miles) to the north is an archipelago of somewhat larger islands, also accessible by boat from the town of Semporna, though the trip is more difficult to arrange as tour companies do not specialize in these islands, which include Sebangkat, Selakan, Maiga,

Map labels: Kota Kinabalu; Boat to Semporna; West Ridge; Wildlife Department; Pulau Sipadan; Jetty; Lobster Lairs; Lighthouse; Dive Centre; Turtle Cavern/tomb; Barracuda Point; Staghorn Crest; Sipadan Marine Park; Coral Gardens; White-tip Avenue; Turtle Patch

Location: Semporna town is at the tip of the most southeasterly peninsula in Sabah, 350 km (218 miles) from Kota Kinabalu and at the extreme opposite side of the state. The Semporna Islands extend to the north and east while Sipadan and Mabul are to the south.

Climate: Hot, often rather dry.

When to Go: Any time of year; expect calmer seas from March–July, and wetter, rougher conditions from October onwards.

Access: By air or overland to Tawau, then by bus or taxi to Semporna. Arrange visits to both Sipadan and Mabul with tour companies prior arrival. Travel to the Semporna Islands can be arranged at Semporna jetty.

Permits: Not required, but those visiting the Semporna Islands should inform the police in Semporna town, giving personal and travel details.

Equipment: Ensure boat owners provide life jackets. Sipadan tour companies should provide all necessities and rent out diving equipment. Visitors to Semporna Islands must take everything, including food and cooking equipment.

Facilities: Huts and dive guides on Sipadan. No facilities on the Semporna Islands. Two dive resorts on Mabul.

Wildlife: Wide range of fish, corals, invertebrates and Coconut Crabs.

Visitor Activities: On Sipadan. Mainly scuba diving at a range of sites round the island.

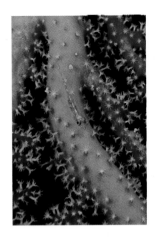

Above: *A camouflaged goby, perched on a fan coral, has an almost transparent body.*

Sibuan, the beautiful Bodgaya, Boheydulang and Tetagan. There is evidence of raised reefs in some areas: Pulau Selangan consists entirely of raised reef limestone, and the town of Semporna is built on an old coral reef, estimated to be around 35,000 years old. Their exposure is due to a general uplifting of the land and surrounding sea bed. Other islands are of volcanic origin. Both Pulau Bodgaya and Boheydulang represent the northern rim of a now flooded and extinct volcanic caldera with the southern rim completely submerged.

Approaching the central islands of Bodgaya, Boheydulang and Tetagan, you will be captivated by the emerald green lagoon sheltered by the surrounding steep cliffs of these three islands. The lagoon is about 8

kilometres (5 miles) across, and the cliffs reach up to 460 metres (1,500 feet) above the sea. The coral reefs here are less colourful than in Sipadan, but may contain more variety. The waters around the islands are clear and warm, and the beaches really are white, especially on Pulau Sibuan.

Getting Around

The best way to appreciate the Semporna Islands is to take a cruise, by renting a small village boat. There are no accommodation facilities on any of the islands, though some are inhabited. On Pulau Maiga there is a community of Taosug people, who have built houses on stilts at the water's edge, from coconut leaves and nipah palm thatch. The men and children here fish for food, and some of the villagers build small boats, apparently from driftwood on the shore. There are

more permanent villages on Pulau Boheydulang and Bodgaya. There is some land clearance here, but most of the resident Bajau Samal and Taosug people are fishermen and so don't need land.

The closest island offering any degree of comfort is Pulau Mabul, halfway between Pulau Sipadan and Semporna, where there is a settlement and chalets built on stilts over the water. Alternatively, it is possible to use Semporna town as a base and make day trips.

Right: *The water's astonishing clarity and the variety of reef life make this area a diver's dream.*

Below: *Fantastically branched and brilliantly coloured colonies of sea fans are prolific here.*

Opposite, below: *A yellow pair of Masked Rabbitfish glide past a superb coral garden.*

ADDRESSES & FURTHER READING

INDIA

**Ministry Environment
& Forests**
Government of India
Pariyavaran Bhawan
Cgo Complex, Lodhi Road,
New Delhi–110003
tel: 91-11-4361669
website: envfor.nic.in
e-mail: secy@menf.delhi.nic.in

Nepal Tourism Board
Tourist Service Centre
Bhrikuti Mandap, Kathmandu
tel: 977-1-256909
website: www.welcomenepal.com
e-mail: info@ntb.wlink.com.np

The Director, Project Tiger
Govt of India, Min. of Environment &
Forests
Bikaner House, Annexe V
Shahjhan Road
New Delhi–110011
tel: 91-11-3384428
website: envfor.nic.in/pt/proj.html
e-mail: dirpt-r@hub.nic.in

World Wide Fund for Nature-India
172-b, Lodhi Estate
New Delhi-110003
tel: 91-11-4633473
e-mail: wwfindel@unv.ernet.in

Ranthambhore Foundation
19, Kautilya Marg
Chanakyapuri
New Delhi–110021
tel: 91-11-3016261;
fax: 11-3019457
website: www.ranthambor.com
e-mail: tiger@vsnl.com

Corbett Foundation
Wildlife Protection Society of India
Thapar House, 124 Janpath
New Delhi–110001
tel: 91-11-3320572
website: www.wpsi-india.org
wpsi@nde.vsnl.net.in

Ibex Expeditions
(Eco tours, adventure, safari travel &
cultural tours)
G66 East of Kailash
New Delhi–110065
tel: 91-11-6912641/7829 or
6828479
website: www.ibexexpeditions.com
e-mail: ibex@nde.vsnl.net.in

**Corbett National Park & Tiger
Reserve**
Chief Conservator Forests,
1, Rana Pratap Marg,
Lucknow–226001

The Field Director
Project Tiger
Corbett Tiger Reserve
Post Office: Ramnagar
Nainital District,
Uttaranchal

**Kaziranga National Park
Reservations**
The Deputy Director, Tourism
PO-Kaziranga Sanctuary
Shibsagar District, Assam
Assam–785109

**Kanha National Park
and Tiger Reserve**
The Field Director
Project Tiger
PO Mandla
Madhya Pradesh

**Bandhavgarh National Park and
Tiger Reserve**
The Manager, White Tiger Forest
Lodge
Madhya Pradesh State Tourism
Development Corporation
Umaria, Shahdol District
Madhya Pradesh

Tourist Officer
Head Office
MPSTDC
4th Floor Gangotri
T T Nagar, Bhopal

**Ranthambhore National Park
and Tiger Reserve**
Field Director, Ranthambhore
National Park and Tiger Reserve
Sawai Madhopur
Rajasthan–322001

**Sunderbans National Park and
Tiger Reserve**
The Field Director
Sunderbans Tiger Reserve
PO Canning
South 24 Parganas District
West Bengal

Gir National Park
The Deputy Conservator of Forests
Wildlife Division
Sasan Gir
Gujarat–362135

**Nagarhole National Park
and Wildlife Sanctuay**
Jungle Lodges and Resorts Limited
2nd Floor
Srinagar Shopping Centre
MG Road
Bangalore–560001

**Periyar National Park
and Tiger Reserve**
Field Director
Project Tiger
Kankikuzhi
Kottayam
Kerala

THAILAND

**Biodiversity Research and
Training Program**
15th Floor Gypsum Tower
539/2 Sri Ayuthaya Road

Rajdhavee
Bangkok 10400
tel: 02 642 5322
e-mail: brt@brtprogram.org
Oriental Bird Club
c/o The Lodge
Sandy
Bedfordshire SG19 2DL
England
e-mail: mail@orientalbirdclub.org

Royal Forest Department
61 Phaholyothin Road
Ladprao
Chatuchak
Bangkok 10900
tel: 02 579 5734
fax: 02 579 9576

Wildlife Fund Thailand
251/88-90 Phaholyothin Road
Bangkhen
Bangkok 10220
tel: 02 521 3435
e-mail: WILDLIFE@mozart.inet.co.th

**World Wide Fund for Nature
Thailand Programme**
104 Outreach Building
AIT
PO Box 4 Klong Luang
Pathumtani, 12120
tel: 02 524 6128-9

THE PHILIPPINES

Department of Tourism
Rm 207, Department of Tourism
Building
TM Kalaw St, Ermita
Manila
tel: 02-5242345

Haribon Foundation
3rd Floor, AM Building
28 Quezon Avenue
Quezon City 1100, Metro Manila
tel: 02-7404989
e-mail: Haribon@phil.gn.apc.org

**National Integrated Protected
Areas Programme (NIPAP)**
Ninoy Aquino Park and Wildlife
Nature Center
North Avenue, Diliman
PO Box 1614, QC-CPO
1156 Quezon City, Metro Manila
tel: 02-9292034
e-mail: asnipap@iconn.com.ph

**Negros Forests and Ecological
Foundation Inc (NFEFI)**
South Capitol Road
Bacolod City 6100
Negros Occidental
tel/fax: 034-4339234

**NGOs for Integrated Protected
Areas (NIPA) Inc**
IPAS-PCU Office
Ninoy Aquino Park and Wildlife
Nature Center
North Avenue, Diliman
Quezon City 1100, Metro Manila
tel: 02-9246031
e-mail: cppappcu@mnl.csi.com.ph

**Palawan Council for Sustainable
Development (PCSD)**
3rd Floor
Capitol Building
Puerto Princesa City, Palawan
tel: 048-4332698

**Protected Areas and Wildlife
Bureau (PAWB)**
Ninoy Aquino Park and Wildlife
Nature Center
North Avenue
Diliman
Quezon City 1100
Metro Manila
tel: 02-9246031

Subic Bay Ecology Centre
Room 220, Building 255
Barryman Road
Subic Bay Freeport Zone 2222
tel: 047-2524435
e-mail: ecology@subic.com.ph

UNESCO National Commission of the Philippines
DFA Building
2330 Roxas Boulevard
Pasay City
Metro Manila
tel: 02-8343447 or 8344844

Whitetip Divers
Units 206/8/9
Joncor II Building
1362 A. Mabini Street
Ermita, Manila
tel: 02-5268190
e-mail: whitetip@info.com.ph

World Wide Fund for Nature (WWF) Philippines
23-A Maalindog Street
UP Village, Diliman
Quezon City 1100, Metro Manila
tel: 02-4333220
e-mail: kkp@mozcom.com

Malaysia

Association of Backpackers Malaysia
No. 6 Jalan SS3/33
47300 Petaling Jaya

Department of Wildlife and National Parks
Km. 10, Jalan Cheras
50664 Kuala Lumpur
tel: 03-9052872
e-mail: kp@jphltn.sains.my

Malaysia Tourism Promotion Board
Floors 24-27, Menara Dato' Onn
Putra World Trade Centre
45 Jalan Tun Ismail
50480 Kuala Lumpur
tel: 03-2935188

Ministry of Culture, Arts and Tourism
Floors 34-36, Menara Dato' Onn
Putra World Trade Centre
45 Jalan Tun Ismail
50694 Kuala Lumpur
tel: 03-2937111

World Wide Fund For Nature (WWF) Malaysia
Locked Bag No. 911
Jalan Sultan PO
46990 Petaling Jaya
tel: 03-7033772
e-mail: wwfmal@pop.jaring.my

National Parks and Wildlife Office Sarawak Forestry Department
Wisma Sumber Alam
Jalan Stadium
Petra Jaya
93660 Kuching
tel: 082-319126

Sarawak Tourism Board
No. 3.43 & 3.44, Level 3, Wisma Satok
Jalan Satok/Kulas
93400 Kuching
tel: 082-423600
e-mail: sarawak@po.jaring.my

Sabah Forest Department
PO Box 311
90007 Sandakan
tel: 089-660811

Sabah Parks
PO Box 10626
88806 Kota Kinabalu

Street address
Block K, Lot 3
Sinsuran Complex
88806 Kota Kinabalu
tel: 088-212508

Sabah Tourism Promotion Corporation
Mail Bag 12
88999 Kota Kinabalu

Street address
51 Jalan Gaya
88000 Kota Kinabalu
tel: 088-218620
e-mail: sabah@po.jaring.my

Sabah Wildlife Department
5th floor, Block B
Wisma MUIS
Sembulan
88300 Kota Kinabalu
tel: 088-214317
e-mail: jhlsabah@tm.net.my

Further Reading India

Ali, Salim and Dillon Ripley, S. (1984) *Compact Handbook Birds of India & Pakistan.* Oxford University Press

Bole, P.V. and Vaghani, Y. (1986) *Field Guide to the Common Trees of India.* Oxford University Press

Corbett, Jim (1944) *Man Eaters of Kumaon.* Oxford University Press

Daniel, J.C. (1983) *The Book of Indian Reptiles.* Bombay Natural History Society

Gee, E.P. (2000) *The Wildlife of India.* Harper Collins

Lal, J.B. (1989) *India's Forests — Myth and Reality.* Natraj Publishers

Prater, S.H. (1948, 1971) *The Book of Indian Animals.* Bombay Natural History Society

Saharia, V.B. (1982) *Wildlife in India.* Natraj Publishers

Further Reading Thailand

Cox, M. J., van Dijk, P. P., Nabhitabhata, J., and Thirakhupt, K. (1998) *A Photographic Guide to Snakes and Other Reptiles of Thailand and South-East Asia.* New Holland Publishers, London.

Gardner, S., Sidisunthorn, P., and Anusarnsunthorn, V. (2000) *A Field Guide to the Forest Trees of Northern Thailand.* Kobfai Publishing Project, Bangkok.

Gray, D., Piprell, C., and Graham, M. (1994) *National Parks of Thailand* (revised edn). Industrial Finance Corporation of Thailand, Bangkok.

Henley, T. (1999) *Reef to Rainforests, Mountains to Mangroves, A Guide to South Thailand's Natural Wonders.* Dawn of Happiness Resort Co., Krabi.

Hutcharern, C., and Tubtim, N. (1995). *Checklist of Forest Insects in Thailand* (vol. 1). Office of Environmental Policy and Planning, Bangkok.

Kekule, L. B. (1999) *Wildlife in the Kingdom of Thailand.* Asia Books, Bangkok.

Lees, P. (1999) *The Dive Sites of Thailand.* Asia Books, Bangkok.

Lekagul, B., and McNeely, J. A. (1988) *Mammals of Thailand* (2nd edn). Saha Karn Bhaet Co. Ltd, Bangkok.

Lekagul, B., and Round, P. D. (1991) *A Guide to the Birds of Thailand.* Saha Karn Bhaet Co. Ltd, Bangkok.

Majchacheep, S. (1989) *Marine Animals of Thailand.* Prae Pittaya Publishers, Bangkok.

Robson, C. (2000). *A Field Guide to the Birds of Thailand and South-East Asia.* New Holland Publishers, London.

Stewart-Cox, B., and Cubitt, G. (1995) *Wild Thailand.* Asia Books, Bangkok.

Further Reading Philippines

Calumpong, H.P. and Menez, E.G. (1997) *Field Guide to the Common Mangroves, Seagrasses and Algae of the Philippines.* Bookmark, Manila

Collar, N.J., Mallari, N.A.D. and Tabaranza, B.R. (1999) *Threatened Birds of the Philippines.* Bookmark, Manila (in association with the Haribon Foundation and BirdLife International)

Fisher, T. and Hicks, N. (2000) *A Photographic Guide to Birds of the Philippines.* New Holland Publishers, London

Gonzalez, J.C.T (1998) *A Pictorial Guide to Philippine Endemic Forest Birds of Mount Makiling, Luzon Island, Philippines.* University of the Philippines at Los Banos Museum of Natural History, Los Banos

Gosliner, T. M., Behrens, D.W. and Williams, G.C. (1996) *Coral Reef Animals of the Indo-Pacific.* Sea Challengers, Monterey, California.

Jackson, J. (1995) *The Dive Sites of the Philippines.* New Holland Publishers, London.

Kuiter, R.H. and Debelius, H. (1997) *Southeast Asia Tropical Fish Guide.* Ikan-Unterwasserarchiv, Frankfurt

Robson, C (2000) *A Field Guide to the Birds of South-east Asia.* New Holland Publishers, London

Further Reading Malaysia

Bernard, H.-U. (1991) *Insight Guide: Southeast Asia Wildlife.* APA Publications, Hong Kong

Bransbury, J. (1993) *A Birdwatcher's Guide to Malaysia.* Waymark Publishing, Australia

Carcasson, R.H. (1977) *A Field Guide to the Reef Fishes of Tropical Australia and the Indo-Pacific Region.* Collins, London and Sydney

Davison, G.W.H. and Chew, Y.F. (1995) *A Photographic Guide to the Birds of Peninsular Malaysia and Singapore.* New Holland Publishers, London

Davison, G.W.H. and Chew, Y.F. (1996) *A Photographic Guide to the Birds of Borneo.* New Holland Publishers, London

Jackson, J. (1995) *The Dive Sites of Malaysia and Singapore.* New Holland Publishers, London

Moore, W. and Cubitt, G. (1995) *This is Malaysia.* New Holland Publishers, London

Payne, J. and Cubitt, G. (1990) *Wild Malaysia: The Wildlife and Scenery of Peninsular Malaysia, Sarawak and Sabah.* New Holland Publishers, London

Payne, J., Cubitt, G and Lau, D. (1994) *This is Borneo.* New Holland Publishers, London

Smythies, B.E. (1981) *The Birds of Borneo* (3rd edn). Sabah Society and Malayan Nature Society, Kota Kinabalu and Kuala Lumpur

Wong, M.P. (1991) *Sipadan: Borneo's Underwater Paradise.* Odyssey Publishing, Singapore

INDEX

PHOTOGRAPHIC ACKNOWLEDGEMENTS

b = bottom, t = top, c = centre, l = left, r = right, f = far

INDIA
Heather Angel: p25(c), p32(t), p44. **Gerald Cubitt**: p12, p13, p14(b), p15 (t,b), p18(c), p20, p21, p22(c), p26, p27, p28(b), p29, p30(bl), p32(b), 34(bl,c,r), p36(fl, fr), p37(b), p41(b), p45(t,b), p49. **Dinodia Photo Library**: p28(tl), p29(tl,r) I. Kehimkar; p36(l), p38, p41(t),p43, p48(b) V. I. Thayil. **Foto Natura**: p36(r) J.Vermeer. **Paul Harris** p46. **Frank Lloyd Picture Agency**: p14(t), p19(br) M. Newman; p15(c), p40(bl) M. Ranjit; p17, p30(tl) D. Hosking; p19(bl) Frank Lane; p22(tl) R. Chittenden; p22(bl), p31, p36(c), p40(br) T.Whittaker; p23 C. Mattison; p25(tl), p33(b) E. & D. Hosking; p25 (tr), p35 T. & P. Gardner; p25(cl) H.D. Brandl; p25(cr) R. Wilsmhurst; p25(br) W.S. Clark; p30(r) M. Withers; p48(t) T. S. V. de Zylva. **Nature, Environment and Wildlife Society**: p37(t).**Toby Sinclair**: p16(t), p18(tr, tl), p19(tr), p24, p28(tr), p32(tr), p33(t), p39, p40(t), p42. **Wilderfile**: p16(b) V. Muthuraman; p33(c) S. Karthikeyan, p47 R.Saravanakumar.

THAILAND
All pictures by **Gerald Cubitt** except the following: **Hans Banziger**: p76(br). **Ron Emmons**: p66(tl,r), p68(b), p69(b). **John Everingham**: p86, p91. **Chew Yen Fook**: p61(b), p73(r). **Jack Jackson**: p89, p90(b). **Bruce Kekule**: p55(t), p60(b), p70(t,b), p71(t), p81.

THE PHILIPPINES
All pictures by **Nigel Hicks** except the following: **Jack Jackson**: p104(b), 105(b), p119.

MALAYSIA
All pictures by **Gerald Cubitt** except the following: **Michael Aw**: p168(tl,r), 168(b), p169(l,r). **Chew Yen Fook**: p136(bl), p154(cl), p156(tr). **Linda Dunk**: p168 (cl). **Martin Edge**: p169, p170(tr). **Jill Gocher**: p149(b), p150, p151, p152(l). **Christopher Gow (Symbiosis Expedition Planning)**: pp152(tr). **Martin Harvey**: p162(tr) **Jack Jackson**: p168(bl). **A. Lamb**: p152(tl). **Malaysian Tourism Promotion Board**: p144(cl). **Jesus Cede Prudente (Wildlife Expeditions)**: p154(r), p160(br), p165(tc,tl,bl). **Raleigh International**: p144(tl). **Struik Image Library (Andrew Bannister)**: p148 (t,c). **Wayne Tarman (Travelcom Asia)**: p153(r). **Arthur Teng**: p144(bl), p158(l). **Albert Teo (Borneo Eco Tours)**: p166(t). **Tham Yau Kong (Borneo Endeavour)**: p158(bl). **Henrietta Van den Bergh**: p165. **Wilderness Photography (Jerry Wooldridge)**: p152(fl), p13(l). **WWF for Nature Malaysia (Azwad M. N.)**: p137.

The Publishers have made every effort to contact and obtain permission from the photographers listed above, to re-use their photographs in this book.